North of Little Hill

North of Little Hill

Proper Talk in
Port Isaac, North Cornwall, 1944–1950

❦

James Platt

Jerusalem on Port Isaac Bay

And did those feet, in hobnailed boots,
Clatter along the playground grey?
And did they from their childhood roots,
On Lobber's skittery cliff swards play?

And did they count their joyous time
On Pine Awn's primrose-dappled hill?
And valley pool, cut withies prime,
Above the dark satanic Mill?

Bring back those days of sunlit gold,
Bring us the hallows they inspire,
With memories dear broad smiles unfold,
Deep in our hearts sweet peace inspire.

From furze girt slopes to marshy brake,
From thundering seas to lug-cast sand,
From glowering cliffs to gurgling Lake,
Port Isaac's green and pleasant land!

With apologies to Mr Willam Blake

This book is dedicated
to the ever precious memory
of my beloved wife Maria

Maria Filomena Platt-Cornoldi
1 January 1941 – 8 July 2008
Requesciat in Pace
Thank you for the Music

Farewell my beautiful!
Thy sinless spirit is with God above.
Thou Hast escaped the evils of the world.
We have a daughter in the Meads of Love
Farewell, my beautiful!

John Harris (1820–1884)
"On the Death of my Daughter Lucretia"

First published in Great Britain in 2009 by Creighton Books
Website: http//www.creightonbooks.nl
Email: jim.platt@planet.nl

© 2009 James Platt

ISBN-10: 90 807808 5 9
ISBN-13: 978 90 807808 5 9

The moral right of James Platt to be identified as the author of this work
has been asserted by him in accordance with
the Copyright, Designs and Patents Act 1988

British Library Cataloguing in Publication Data
A catalogue record for this book is available from the British Library

Designed in the UK by Special Edition Pre-Press Services
Printed and bound in Great Britain by Lightning Source UK Ltd

Also by James Platt and published by Creighton Books

East of Varley Head – Stories from Port Isaac, North Cornwall 1945–1950
(Published in 2003, ISBN 90807808 1 2)

Your Reserves or Mine?
(Published in 2004, ISBN 90 807808 2 0)

South of Lobber Point – More stories from Port Isaac, North Cornwall 1945–1950
(Published in 2005, ISBN 90 807808 3 9)

The Great Tanganyika Diamond Hunt
(Published in 2007, ISBN 978 90 807808 4 2)

List of Illustrations

Acknowledgements

This book was designed and prepared throughout by Corinne Orde and Romilly Hambling who together form the media service company Special-Edition Pre-Press Services (www.special-edition. co.uk). The kindness, level of style, expertise and patience that they lavished on the book were exemplary. Corinne's skill in editing and definitively improving the work added so much to the final version that it could not have been of greater benefit.

The book was digitally set and registered for print-on-demand orders with key trade and Internet booksellers and distributors by Lightning Source UK Limited of Milton Keynes (www. lightningsource.com). LSUK's total commitment to Creighton Books showed a consistent professional excellence and personal consideration that could not be bettered.

I am very much in the debt of all those Port Isaac people from the late 1940s, characters one and all, who are named in the book. It was a privilege for me to have spent my childhood in their company and an entire pleasure to be now able to commemorate them on the printed page. Some of them are happily still with us to this day. Should there be anyone omitted from mention who rightly ought to have been included, this is entirely due to the shortcomings of my memory and for that I apologise to all concerned, including you the reader.

A special acknowledgement is due to my good friend Mike Ferrett. We were fellow-pupils at Sir James Smith's Grammar School, Camelford, North Cornwall, from 1950 to 1957. The idea for a book such as this was suggested by Mike over lunch one day in London in 2005, and I am most indebted to him for it.

Finally, I would like to thank from the bottom of my heart my beloved wife Maria for her unfailing support during the formative stages of this book. She passed away before its completion, but her beauty of spirit will never leave me.

Introduction

The playground flowed around the Port Isaac County Primary School buildings in what resembled a tight horseshoe-like meander. According to village sages, of whom there were many (far too many, as far as any Port Isaac boy worth his salt would ever wish to admit), a horseshoe symbolised good luck.

Few boys who tramped and pounded the playground's tough surface, however, would have been inclined to acknowledge good luck as a grace affecting their everyday lives. Whatever they did, whether at school or at home, they just knew that there would always be some miserable old interfering bugger too close to hand with interests that didn't coincide with theirs.

As it was, one stretch of the playground coming off the back curve was significantly shorter than the other, on the strength of which the general configuration could well have been likened to the rudiments of the letter J. As J was the first letter of my Christian name, this comparison appealed to me as a most acceptable alternative to a U-shaped horseshoe.

Time winnows grains of good wheat from a preponderance of chaff to ensure that late harvests of school memories are always of palatable quality. Notwithstanding this rose-coloured truth, he who first declared that his school days were the happiest of his life and thereby institutionalised a homily to be hotly contested by boys, not to mention girls, for ever and a day to come, would have got short shrift had he expounded this opinion in the Port Isaac County Primary School playground back in the 1940s when I tramped, slid, fought and fell regularly on its gritty tarmac. The very least sanction that he would have been subjected to would have involved forcible transfer by some of the big boys to the cloakroom at the back of the school for a game of "roughhouse". The mazed sod would then soon have seen fit to revise his view to offer us something sounding a little less smug.

That playground (whether horseshoe or J, it was always most hallowed in memory) was subdivided into two distinctive sectors thanks to the insertion of a venerable ten-feet high transverse wall. The wall was constructed from thick, over-leafy slate blocks, no doubt quarried locally, that were held in questionable stability by friable mortar. The flaking cleavage of the slate block faces was a function of their exposure both to the attrition of wind and weather and the steady assault of the hobnail booted feet of would-be climbers from either side. No small boy could ever consider himself secure on one side of the wall if there was a big boy on the other side whom he had affronted and who was intent on revenge. The wall, which more or less bisected the tight curve of the playground at the back end of the school, was a far from inviolate barrier.

The smaller of the two wall-separated playground sectors was designated exclusively for the use and alleged protective containment of the school's so-called infants' class. It formed the floor of a rather dank pit sandwiched between the inland facing side of the school and Fore Street, Port Isaac's principal artery leading to the downtown part of the village. Fore Street was such that, to paraphrase the famous *News of the World* slogan, it could truly be affirmed that "all human life was there".

2

The infants' class was the lowest ranking of four classes which stacked up to form the school's academic (if such a word could be associated with Port Isaac County Primary) hierarchy. Pupils entered the infants' class aged four or five and left to step up to the next class level on reaching the age of seven. The age ranges of pupils in the other three classes were respectively seven to nine, nine to eleven, and eleven to fifteen. The latter considered themselves to be the school's elite—all lower mortals were subject to their will. They were from the headmaster's class, which was always referred to in deference to the nickname of the much revered headmaster of the day as "Boss's class". "Boss" was Mr C. Victor Richards, a man regarded by every pupil with a level of respect verging on Messianic awe.

Boss invigilated the larger sector of playground where all plus seven year olds gave vent in two fifteen-minute break periods per day to an impressive surge of mayhem that was sometimes organised but which more often than not was decidedly ad hoc. Boss's consistency was legendary. He never broke up a playground fight if one of his favourites was judged by him as shaping up to be the likely winner.

This outer boundary of this sector of playground flanked the harbour-facing redoubt of the school buildings and extended onwards past the blind red brick edge of the Old Lifeboat House to terminate against the back wall of a sheltered cliff-side enclave named Little Hill, where gossips were wont to congregate for pontification purposes for just as long as what Gran Creighton called "God's good daylight" held sway.

Little Hill came as close as was humanly possible, notwithstanding that the Port Isaac Town Platt performed an equivalent role, to fulfilling mandatory village public forum duties. Within its comforting embrace any noted gossip, yarn spinner or bullshitter could expound at length on how little he or she knew, waxing and waning in intensity in accordance with the dictates of the moment. Anyone anxious to know, as the local expression went, "the ins and outs of the cat's asshole" would be certain to gain solace of mind on Little Hill.

Conveniently located on the side of Fore Street, about half way down or up, depending on your direction of precedence, Little Hill was a sort of compact abutment pushing hard against a low wall at the edge of the harbour cliff and commanding an unparalleled view of Roscarrock Hill on the harbour's far side. The other great assets of this blessed retreat were the Ladies' Public Lavatory bordering on the downhill front, and adjacent to the Ladies entry, a chute piercing the retaining wall through which all imaginable manner of domestic spoil could be dumped into the embrace of the cleansing tide below.

The boundary of Boss's sector of playground on the side that really counted was a wall which, in common with its Little Hill extension, was no more than a yard high, and almost as broad. The wall faithfully followed the very rim of the harbour cliff, surmounting a sheer drop of at least fifty feet down to the harbour-side rocks, with little more than a tortured fringe of blackthorn bushes offering a doubtful barrier to hold whatever went over the wall either by accident or design.

It was not merely expected but also very much mandatory that once in a while, big boy predators from Boss's class were going to cross the dividing wall to raid the infants' playground precincts. This was welcomed by smaller boys in the main playground sector as it gave them a respite, albeit temporary, from thememselves being forced to submit to the big boys' whims and wiles.

The narrowest spot in the bigger sector of playground was located between a front corner buttress of the school building and the cliff-edge wall. This virtual bottleneck was no more than ten feet wide, serving to separate two regions, each of which was a recognised territorial reserve in its own right. The more restricted back region, known as "in-around", was where small boys did their best to lurk in anonymity during playtime in the hope of avoiding active contact with the big boys. The latter traditionally favoured the open ranges of the front region, known as "out-around". It was on the hard field of battle of out-around that raging football contests incorporated anything with a rounded shape that could be kicked (not stopping short of small boys' backsides) and during which regular sessions of fisticuffs served as everyday punctuation marks to settle disputes.

To spice up the action a few of the big boys (they took it in turns) were assigned by order of the recognised leaders of their company of stalwarts to link arms so as to form a human barricade sealing the playground bottleneck. Their counterparts then rounded up all the small boys they were able to quickly intimidate, time being of the essence, in order to drive the small boys at the barricade like a herd of stampeding cattle in what was an inevitably failed endeavour to break through. This undecorous game was known by the ponderous title of "the big ones keep the little ones in-around".

"What larks!" as Joe Gargery was given to remarking to Pip. The problem that small Port Isaac boys were burdened with was that, unlike Pip, they had no cause to believe that any great expectations awaited them on this side of the grave.

So there it stood, and for what it was worth it was worth a lot, the school on the edge of the cliff; its rambling playground with a slate wall that was as divisive as it was dividing; and the tag-on haven named Little Hill. All of this was an entity that was much greater than the sum of its parts—being no more and no less than the hub of the pupils' known world. It wove its magic erratically in a welter of wagging tongues, flying fists, sudden impacts, skinned knees, bloody noses, ripped-out tufts of hair and a pervasive clatter of hobnails. Its richness lay in the warp and weft of the rolling dialect of its key actors and bit players alike, generating humour as raw as it was uproarious, manifest in a compendium of original yarns, rhymes and dictates of which any literary tradition could have been justifiably proud.

Any boy (or girl) who attended the Port Isaac County Primary School as a pupil during the late 1940s will have no hesitation from the vantage point of sixty years on to tell anyone impressed into listening to him (or her) that he (or she) dearly loved not only the school but also its teachers and all that they stood for. Since the teachers had little alternative other than to stand for the pupils it can be accepted that what they stood for was pretty much anything. Notwithstanding this truth, back in those immediate post-war days when retrospection counted for nothing, any declaration by a pupil of affection for school or teachers was as rare as chough eggs on Lobber cliff.

Port Isaac during that halcyon period was a native community existing in rural isolation on the rugged coast of North Cornwall, where it stewed in its own far less than fragrant juice. Local inbreeding was the order of the day, although the same thing was a standard demographic feature in any other North Cornish, or for that matter Cornish village. The people of Port Isaac conducted their own business in their own way, and if it wasn't the best way in the judgement of others, then it certainly wasn't for the want of not trying.

The population of the village contained more genuine characters per unit of dwelling area than a shitty stick could be shaken at. As far as the Port Isaac boys of the time were concerned, shitty sticks brandished in the hoary fists of those said characters, not to mention in the raised and threatening hands of the boys' elders and betters, were all too frequently shaken in their direction at little more than the drop of any one of those character's sweat-stained, fish scale-garlanded flat cap.

Everyday life balanced evenly on the fulcrum of a simplistic two-layered social structure, which consisted of Us and Them—respectively the Likes of We and the Likes of They.

The Likes of We bowed our heads and touched our forelocks to the Likes of They in grudging acknowledgement of their self-serving and self-appointed superiority over us. In the school playground hierarchy the Likes of We were the pupils—the Likes of They were our ubiquitous figures of authority. Among the pupils, age was held to be directly proportional to status, yet for all that we rallied resolutely as one against the common enemy.

By comparison with the Likes of We, the Likes of They were few in number. They tweaked strings hoping to induce us to dance in ready compliance to their tune. Most of the Likes of They were from parts outside the sphere of influence of the village, and hence were foreigners of one kind or another. They seemed duty bound to ensure that the Likes of We never forgot our place in the great scheme of things. As the leather-tough Mrs Emmeline (Em) Kent of Port Isaac's Hartland Road once said to me, "The Likes of They buggers talks different to the Likes of We."

Dear old Em's comment set out in precise terms the principle expounded by that plummy mouthed Likes of They bugger Professor Henry Higgins who declared in Shaw's *Pygmalion*, "It is impossible for an Englishman to open his mouth without making some other Englishman hate or despise him!"

It was really quite straightforward. The Likes of They accepted grovelling servitude from the Likes of We more or less as their divine right. When I think about this, I don't take any issue with the malign aspects of the nature of far too many of the Likes of They, since they were just as much victims of birth and circumstance as were we, but their penchant for blocking the opportunities we might have had to rise above what they regarded as our allotted station of subservience to them in life was so desperately and knowingly unfair that I find it unforgivable.

For all that, the Likes of We rejoiced in our locally accented manipulation of the English language. The broader the accent, the more culturally satisfying for us was the result. We spoke soft and slow, drawing long on our vowels, and rolling our discourse like a mighty Atlantic swell. We adopted our accent as an integral part of learning to speak, cherishing the developments of dialect in the streets, and honing the finer points in the fertile pit of that great social leveller, the school playground.

The boys of Port Isaac were a tribal unit. We had to be tough, and all of us were tough enough. The school playground was the core of our territory. The Likes of They induced us to believe that our manifest destiny was to eke out our lives within the vicinity of the village, in keeping with which our cultural imperative tended not to look at the world anywhere beyond the immediate local environment. Strength was reckoned to outweigh intellect on any day of the week. Since ignorance was bliss, the most heinous folly any one of us could commit was to try to be wise. Hence we conducted our daily affairs in a time-honoured tradition, and drew up our tongues to sound all our "r's" when speaking as if that very letter was placed in the alphabet for no reason other than to define us.

My seeds were firmly planted in the blooming garden of the Likes of We, and to this day I couldn't be more proud that they were.

I was cast adrift from the safe haven of the Port Isaac County Primary School playground as a consequence of passing a so-called "eleven-plus" examination (which curiously enough I had to take when I was still ten years old). It could have merited a panel discussion at the outset as to whether my success had rewarded or condemned me into subsequently attending the grandly named Sir James Smith's Grammar School located eleven miles away from Port Isaac in the all too sombre town of Camelford. At that fount of education, commonly referred to as the Camelford Grammar School, or better yet the CGS, I was subjected to the shock of contact with a whole host of strangers, namely fellow-pupils hailing from wildly foreign settlements of the North Cornwall district such as Tintagel, Boscastle, St Kew, Delabole, St Teath, St Breward, Camelford itself, Davidstow and so on and bewilderingly so forth.

I carried my Port Isaac accented dialect along with me—it would take a few years of attending the CGS to rub away a little of the tough shell of my enduring allegiance to Port Isaac and all things thereof. Equal considerations could be applied to Boscastle boys, or Tintagel boys, or boys from any of the other places, although it went without saying that Port Isaac boys would always be the best of the bunch.

Unfortunately, any manifestation of a boy's pride in his indigenous roots did not sit too well with certain of the CGS teachers. Those worthies seemed motivated to single out certain individuals as receptacles into which they could pour their disdain. The eternal battle between the Likes of We and the Likes of They was by no means unknown at the CGS.

Miss Phyllis White, who taught English, was a florid-faced spinster who, although not yet knocking on the door of being middle-aged, seemed to be always hovering on the verge of turning into an imperious old maid. She appeared to take a special delight in casting the native tone of my speech into a figurative river where she could pound it on the rocks before throwing it out to dry on the banks. Miss White was nicknamed "Polly". Jane Austen would have recognised her type in an instant.

As I was a good student of her subject, Polly's aggressive assault on my accent felt to me to be as mean as it was unreasonable. I might have blossomed under a more sympathetic English teacher. As it was, the light that I emitted soon became firmly overshadowed by Polly's bushel.

Her technique involved firing sudden questions at me that she knew I would find difficult to answer and so result in my ending up a tongue-tied figure good for a cheap laugh. For an English Lit encore, Polly liked to make me to read a passage which she selected for effect from her currently set class book. With this ploy she got me to add spice to her day by offering her numerous opportunities to engage in mockery. I imagined she saw herself as a sort of Max Miller (minus the Blue Book gags) working the class with the thrust of her sarcastic repartee.

I eventually decided that if this kind of performance was what Polly wanted from me then I would play along as the "straight man" butt of her jibes. I consciously broadened my accent. As a gesture of defiance this was counterbalanced by an ever-diminishing self esteem. In the end I simply chose to act mute, and although this only served to emphasise my inadequacy as far as Polly was concerned, she did finally leave me to my own devices, weighted down with a Port Isaac accent that had thus far travelled neither far nor well.

Polly held all the key cards. She marked me low in every English examination I took which she set. It was fortunate that my English exam at "O" level was marked by an external examiner since he (or she) saw fit to award me the top grade for my efforts. This annoyed Polly no end.

My accent-loaded impasse with her petered out in stalemate—a Mexican standoff worthy of any Port Isaac Rivoli cinema B-movie western in stark black and white. As it was neither Polly nor I survived the shoot-out with the least touch of glory intact.

It spoke heavy volumes of the English Lit kind which Polly favoured having me read from that a Cornish accent featured more by accident than design in BBC wireless broadcasting of that time—or for that matter in theatrical performances, in the cinema, or on that budding innovation called "telly-vision". A Cornish voice heard on the air was invariably being used to characterise a rural hayseed, a village idiot or a smock-clad local yokel, all subjects of derisory fun.

It came as no surprise to me at all that when I left the CGS in 1957 and went off to far flung foreign parts to study at the Imperial College of London University, a common reaction of people I met and spoke to for the first time was a meaningful look, an "Oo, Arr" expression, and an attempt at the kind of Long John Silver eye-roll that Robert Newton had made famous.

All of the oo-ing and arr-ing probably heralded a last desperate throw of the dice for detractors of spoken Cornish dialect. Rural society was evolving under the rising ease of personal mobility; the availability of the ever-expanding information media; and quite importantly a diminution of respect, as welcome as it was justified, by the Likes of We for Likes of They authority.

A death knell for the impending demise of local accent and dialect in North Cornwall is ringing in most of the county's twenty-first century primary schools. Pupil tribalism is gone, playgrounds have been tamed, and the bland neutrality of English taught with received pronunciation reigns supreme. It seems more than probable that in the time of a generation or two from now, local dialect and accent will have achieved its final extinction.

On a certain day at the end of my first year as a student at Imperial College I was on my way to Newcastle by train. A few years previously the mere thought of my going to a place as foreign as Newcastle (carrying coals or not) would have been too frightening for me to have contemplated. For that matter, it didn't much appeal to me on the train either. My purpose in travelling to Newcastle was to connect with a ferry to Bergen in Norway.

When the train stopped at York station, a young man who looked to be in his mid-twenties took a seat opposite me in the compartment in which I had until then been the sole passenger.

From his demeanour and the well-nigh tangible aura of beer that preceded him by a good couple of yards, I surmised that a substantial number of pints had played a role in his recent life. Once he was seated following a rather ungainly manoeuvre, he proceeded to talk more or less non-stop all the way to Newcastle. The train's arrival at that final destination bestowed upon me the true blessing of relief that only escape from torment can bring.

My ability to throw a word in edgeways was compromised by the pace of his discourse. Apart from my gathering from his accent that he was of rock-solid Geordie stock, and of my reaching an understanding that he had that very day emerged from two weeks of enjoyable incarceration in a Butlin's holiday camp located at Filey, almost all that he said to me was so incomprehensible that it might as well have been delivered in ancient Greek.

What was equally undeniable was that even if I had managed to break into his monologue, his response on listening to me would have been no different from my reaction to hearing him. We were two people from opposing poles of the same country, two compatriots alienated by dialect.

To be as diplomatic as possible I did my best to nod sagely at the Geordie's every utterance. He seemed to take this as encouragement to expound ever further on the obtuseness of his Butlin's experiences. It was a telling encounter. Our regional accents were living on borrowed time.

This book offers the reader, in the form of a glossary, a record of many of the dialect terms and expressions in common use among Port Isaac boys (as well as their elders and betters) in the years immediately succeeding the Second World War. I don't lay any claim to the treatment being definitive, but trust that the record will provide a broad base of elements of a rich spoken heritage that is fast fading.

The scheme adheres very much to a Port Isaac context—the listing is alphabetic and the dialect terms are defined and illustrated with examples of their application as heard in everyday conversation of the day. Such conversations took place on the village streets, in the school playground, on the benches at Little Hill, down on the harbour beach, out along the cliffs, on and around the Town Platt, in the shops—in short, anywhere at all that the Likes of We congregated to conduct our social gossip and our business or to participate in one of the few pleasures that the Likes of They granted to us.

Some of the provided examples consist of informal rhymes and chants that grew from hesitant seedlings into sturdy plants on the darkly rich surface of the Port Isaac County Primary School playground.

The reader who elects to work his or her way through the glossary and practise getting his or her tongue around the examples is likely to be interested in a few phonetic rules on pronunciation technique.

The rules aren't many, and here they are!

- Sound the letter R wherever you see it.
- Drop every H that falls at the start of a word, although there are some exceptions (see Glossary entries under "H").
- Elongate all vowels, especially A.
- The letters V or Ph at the start of a word can be pronounced as if they were an F and vice versa.
- An S at the start of a word can often be pronounced as if it was a Z.

That should more or less do it!

Port Isaac Primary School
1947–1948
Class Photographs

The Infants' Class (Age 4 to 7)

Left to Right—Back Row: Priam Thomas; Tommy (Ducks Egg) Bradshaw; Trevor Platt; Graham Taylor; Peter-John Graham; Tony Collins; Anthony Angell; (Unknown); David Thomas. *Middle Row:* Nora Keat; Georgina Williams; (Unknown); Christine Glover; Anthea Bessell; Jeanette Honey; Anne Julian; Eileen Bunt. *Front Row:* Maxine Derbyshire; (Unknown); Betty Chadband; Audrey Collings; Joy Collins; (Unknown); Barbara Thomas

The Second Class (Age 7 to 9)

Left to Right—Back Row: Roger Perry; Barwis Bennett; Michael (Eyesnot) Bate; Maxie Richards; Francis (Joey) Thomas. *Middle Row:* Mollie Hooke; Roger Keat; Leonard (Buh) Honey; James Platt; Colin Mitchell; June Mitchell; Merle Honey. *Front Row:* Vera Tamsett; Vivienne Donnithorne; Margaret Blake; Mrs Morman (Class Teacher); Ann Thomas; Brenda Hawkey; Pat Tucker.

15

The Third Class (Age 9 to 11)

Left to Right—Back Row: David Sloggett; Ronald (Mo) Tamsett; Peter Wright; Michael (Cogsy) Collings; Dudley (Monk) Taylor; Barrie Wright; Gordon (Arker) Keat; Michael Vagges. *Middle Row:* Eileen Byfield; Marguerite Keat; Esme Hawkey; Veronica Keat; Tony Ball; Joe Knight; Terry (Tibby) Thomas; Doreen Byfield; Pearl Honey; (Unknown). *Front Row:* Velma Collings; Janet Sweet; Roberta Derbyshire; Thelma (Stink Bomb) Bennett; Diane Mitchell; Betty Bracey; Virginia Thomas; Georgina Hocking; Jean Glover.

The Headmaster's Class (Age 11 to 15)

Left to Right—Back Row: Fred Vagges; Jack Clemmow; Brian (Marshall) Blake; Warren (Flynn) Dinner; Len Pluckrose; Alan Chadband; Derek Pooley; Brian (Pills) Richards; Tony Blake *Middle Row:* Bertie Byfield; (Unknown); Brian (Otch) Orchard; Richard Couch; Tony (Dick) Derbyshire); Raymond (Ido) Glover. *Front Row:* Mabel Thomas; Nora Gregory; Mildred Thomas; Harriet Glover; Joyce Masters; Maureen Glover; Shirley Derbyshire.

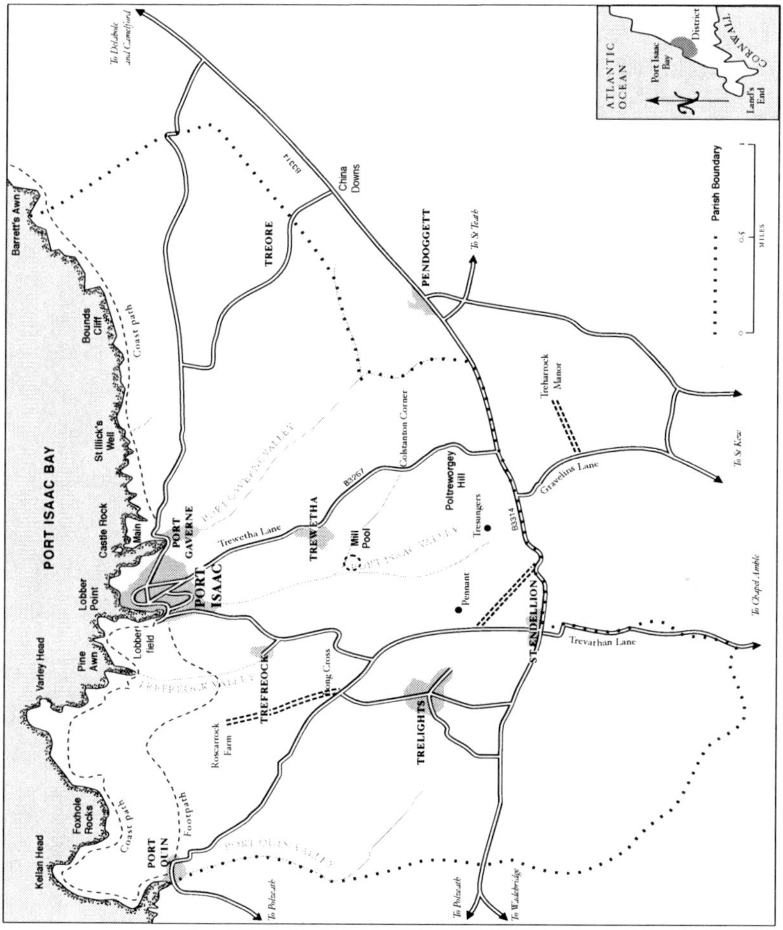
PORT ISAAC BAY
Kellan Head
Foxhole Rocks
Varley Head
Pine Awn
Lobber Point
Castle Rock
Main
St Illick's Well
Bounds Cliff
Barrett's Awn
Coast path
Coast path
Footpath
PORT QUIN
Lobber field
PORT ISAAC
PORT GAVERNE
TREFREOCK
Roscarrock Farm
Long Cross
TRELIGHTS
Trewetha Lane
TREWETHA
B3267
Mill Pool
Colstanton Corner
Poltreworgey Hill
Tresungers
Pennant
B3314
ST ENDELLION
Trevathan Lane
TREORE
China Downs
B3314
PENDOGGETT
To St Teath
Treharrock Manor
Gravelins Lane
To St Kew
To Chapel Amble
To Polzeath
To Polzeath
To Wadebridge
To Delabole and Camelford
Parish Boundary
0
0.5
1
MILES
ATLANTIC OCEAN
Port Isaac Bay
District
CORNWALL
Land's End

The Glossary

A

A

Pronounced as if it were an indefinite article (which more than a few long-suffering Port Isaac housewives would reckon to be not without good reason), *a* is the common version of the third person singular pronoun as applied to identifying a bona fide member of the male sex. A reasonable alternative for *a* is *un*—some villagers consider that switching to *un* is mandatory when the word following hard on the heels of *a* commences with either a vowel or an aspirate aich (not that an aspirate aich counts for much, as Port Isaac men invariably drop it as enthusiastically as they abandon any thoughts about work being a good thing).

> *"Where be a to?"*
> *"Ah dun't knaw nart 'bout un, en ah dun't care where th' bugger do be s'long ez tedden 'ere!"*

Abroad

A word with two distinctive meanings:

(1) An unbecoming situation involving clothing left undone or gaping open or rent asunder, either following a mishap or

by design. Loose shirt tails, unfastened coat and fly buttons, broken collar studs, failed braces and fatigued knicker elastic are common ever-present factors to clothes seen to be all *abroad*. One should not, however, rule out the contributory cause of carelessness in creating the effect, as for example in the aftermath of a hastily taken piddle or bowel movement, not least if one or the other (or both) occurred behind a bush.

> *"Do ee knaw yer flies do be all abroad?"*
> *"Dun't think ah do, but ef ee wuz t' 'um th' toon ah'll tell ee."*

(2) A place located anywhere in those dark and mysterious territories which exist everywhere beyond the accepted borders of the parish of St Endellion and which are known to be populated almost exclusively by foreigners.

> *"Where be th' vicar to?"*
> *"A've gone abroad, in t' Waybridge."*

Adam's Aale

A clear and essentially tasteless liquid which falls from the sky as rain, gurgles along the Port Isaac and Port Gaverne valley bottoms in streams, is emitted from taps, descends into your bedroom via the ceiling when a sudden thaw follows a severe freeze-up of the tank up in the loft, and which according to scientists is equipped with a chemical formula sounding something like aich-too-oh. Overtly favoured as the beverage of choice by chapel people, there are many followers of other religious persuasions who consider their personal liquid intake should contain a certain amount of cee-too-aich-five-oh-aich mixed with their *Adam's aale*. They choose to avoid imbibing *Adam's aale* on its own thank you very much, as they all profess to be too well aware of the indisputable fact that fish fornicate in it.

20

> *"They chapel paypull, they zay they do drink only Adam's aale,*
> *but they'm purty nuff fer th' 'arder stuff when they goes abroad*
> *t' plaaces where nobuddy dun't knaw uv em."*

Addick

A species of fish. As this fish is taken from the sea by the fishermen of Port Isaac only on rare occasions, imported *addick* is made available for purchase from itinerant fish *jouders* of the parish. These worthies offer the *addick* to their wealthier customers in portions tinted yellow owing to the fish having been allegedly smoked. Sad to relate, it seems that most *addick* ends up on breakfast tables laid for the delectation of gentry.

> *"Er gived we a dish uv tay, en ah tell ee twuz s' weak ez*
> *addick's water. Ah tole 'er t' taake ut 'way—ah kin piddle*
> *stronger'n that ah zaid!"*

Aff

Each portion of a single entity subdivided into two equal parts is described as a *aff*. Exactness of bisection is particularly critical in instances involving items of food, since even a minimal indication of inequality of partition (which Port Isaac boys are expert in assessing at a glance) can set siblings at one another's throats.

> *"Ah dun't want that payce, ah do want t' ev th' biggest 'aff!"*

Affnoon

Affnoon covers the part of each and every day that commences when the clock strikes twelve noon and ends whenever evening is deemed to have arrived. The noble truth that dinner-time coincides with the starting-point of *affnoon* does much to ease the burden of boys forced to endure the one p.m. to four p.m. wasteland of school that always rushes in far too hard on the termination of their dinner.

"Ah dun't mind guyne t' church in th' marnin, but ah aates evin' t' be there in th' affnoon, speshly when tez fer Zundy skool."

Afower

The embodiment of precedence, manifest whenever something is recognised to have come along before something else. For example, if you should think it prudent to undertake one particular action prior to carrying out a second action (subject to the successful completion of the first), the initial action, irrespective of its complexity, will have taken place *afower* the second.

"Ah be guyne t' 'ev 'nother pint afower ah goes 'ome. Oo's guyne buy un fer me?"

Ah

Ah yes! *Ah* is the standard first person singular device by which you are enabled to make direct reference to your own identity. *Ah* offers evidence that you were born, are still in the land of the living, and are stuck with one or more Christian names and a surname that, whether you like it or not, you can do nothing about.

"Ah do think, therefoo-er ah be!"

With apologies to Descartes

Aid

An *aid* is a rounded appendage at the top of a neck. Its contents have been variously described as consisting of either a brain, an empty void, pure bone or solid timber. An *aid* is encased in skin and pierced by seven orifices that are individually designed to support the senses of sight, taste, smell and hearing. It is capped by hair which comes along in a range of singular hues, some being natural and some not.

In the absence of an *aid*, not only would it be impossible for you to eat, but barbers and dentists among others would experience great difficulty in making a living.

> "Ah do declare ah dun't knaw what be guyne on inzide th' 'aid uv ee!"

Aig

A thick and variegated fluid contained within an impermeable thin and brittle shell of ovoid shape is what constitutes an *aig*. *Aigs* are generated by female birds in a species-distinctive range of sizes, relative shapes, background colour and markings. The *aigs* of so-called wild birds are much collected by Port Isaac boys—small wonder that such birds are wild. The contents of the shell of a commercial variety of *aig* derived from the domestic fowl is a cooking staple. The acquisition of a few chicken's *aigs* (gulls' *aigs* make a useful substitute in season) offers an opportunity for bacon and *aigs* to be prepared for breakfast, provided bacon is also available.

> Fust aig uv th' zayzun;
> Aw, what a s'prize!
> Us dedden think us'd git wan;
> But we'm thinking lies!

With many thanks to Mr Leonard "Buh" Honey of the Old Council Houses

Air

A softly fibrous substance, pleasing to the touch and (what cannot be too strongly stressed yet again) essential to the well-being of barbers, *air* covers the top of the *aid* of anyone who isn't bald, and is often at its sparsest on babies.

> "Ed'n ut bout time that ee waished yer 'air?"

23

"Cert'n'ly not, ah done ut only a fortnight back!"

In fond appreciation of Mr William John Honey, master barber of Fore Street, who styled gentlemen's hair to order, provided the order was for a "shoo-ertbackinzidesenzumofffthutop"

Ait

Ait is used to express a mildly negative connotation when you wish to imply that an action demanded of you may perhaps be fulfilled in the course of time, although with no guarantees placed by you on when it will actually get consummated. In other words, where *ait* is concerned, immediate action pending is unlikely to be the order of the day.

> *"Ev ee done what ah told ee t' do?"*
> *"Ah eb'm done ut ait, but ah'll do ut dreckly."*

Aiz

As the ultimate affirmation, *aiz* signifies full agreement and ready acceptance of the same. In a time-saving alternative to *aiz* some Port Isaac men consider it acceptable to simply purse their lips while drawing a short but audible breath through the thereby restricted channel of their mouths. The greater the sibilance the better the positive understanding will be.

> *"Would ee like t' scraape th' rice puddin dish?"*
> *"Aiz playze!"*

Along

Any known place or location is by definition either up, down, in or out *along* somewhere or other with respect to a known point of reference—in the case of Port Isaac the reference point is likely to be the back door of someone's cottage home. *Up along* then points to somewhere located either to the north of the reference point or at a higher elevation to it. By contrast, *down along* requires thinking in either more southerly or less elevated terms. The group of men who wanted to go to Widdecombe fair on Tom Pearce's grey mare were, however, confusingly uncertain about their bearings if their lament *"all along, down along, out along lea"* is to be believed.

> *"Where did ee git they luv'ly blackberries maid?"*
> *"Aw, up along th' bottoms, t'other zide uv Tom Saundry's archard!"*

In appreciation of the legendarily cantankerous Mr Tom Saundry of Middle Street

Ancient

A quality applied to a person or a thing aimed at registering not only that he, she or it is much admired, but also that what he, she or it is merits unstinting approval. To be *ancient* does not necessarily require the attainment of a venerable age.

> *"Whadoo ee think uv th' noo taychur down be th' skool?"*
> *"Caw, a be zome ancient buhy, ben't a!"*

Anns

Your *anns* (singular *ann*) are a pair of extremely versatile and articulate appendages located out at the ends of your arms, each *ann* being equipped with five digits (comprising four fingers and a thumb). Without *anns* to apply to pleasurable tasks such as picking your nose or scratching your backside, not only would there be a recognisable void created in your life, but Mr Max Bygraves would have missed out on one of his most enduringly popular songs. Each of your *anns* features a flat part known as a palm from which the five digits radiate. It is reliably claimed that certain natural lineations marking the palm can, when examined by a self-confessed expert, be used to interpret precisely how bleak your future is likely to be.

> *"That bugger do be s' thick in a's aid that a cudden find a's haass if a ad dree anns t' look fer un with."*

Ansum

A word of enormous significance in Cornish culture, incorporating as it does marked sentiments of endearment. *Ansum* is normally invoked by more mature members of the population of Port Isaac, whether male or female, in addressing either their male contemporaries or much younger to relatively younger members of the male sex. In principle, neither age nor physical appearance places any constraint on when and where *ansum* may be applied, as it is perfectly in order to address the word to an aged subject whose looks could curdle milk.

> *"Allo mah ansum, 'ow luvly tez t' zee ee!"*
> *"Ah jus' wish ah could zay th' zaame fer ee missis!"*

Argyfyin

This word expresses a contumacious state of verbal exchange which is entered into irrespective of the grounds for doing so being spurious or sound. *Argyfyin* is accepted by most Port Isaac folk as an important ingredient to enhance the elixir of their lives. Without *argyfyin* to rely on as a boost to the spirits, many of its practitioners would in all likelihood have been long since sent up to *Endellion* in a *wood overcoat* to push up daisies from an earth-enveloped resting place six feet under. And on the strength of that, who is there to say that *argyfyin* is not a good thing?

> *"Dun't ee go too neer ol' mother Baaker's front gardin buhy, er's always up fer comin' out after ee en argyfyin' like a terror."*

Ark

An exclamation embodying enough amazement to verge on incredulity, *ark* is most likely to be ejaculated by someone shortly after he or she has observed taking place a situation or event providing fodder for the imagination.

> *"Will ee ark at they shoes er do be wearin'!"*
>
> *"Th' las' time ah zeed they shoes they wuz on th' vit uv 'er Aunt Jinny when that poor ol' maid wuz stretched out daid on th' kitchin taable afower 'er wuz ayved in 'er coffin en scrooed down."*
>
> *"Ark et ee! They dun't look much do em, but they'm better off on livin' vit than bein left on Aunt Jinny zecks vit down!"*

Arry Frampton

Just who the redoubtable *Mr Arry Frampton* actually was has been lost in the mist of both time and memory. The possibility exists that he may have been a disciple of the equally celebrated Mr Heath Robinson. One thing is certain—*Arry Frampton* would have been an expert at creating fudged solutions to tasks and problems. As far as is known, no situation or challenge was either too simple or too complex to receive *Arry Frampton's* sub-standard attention. The tradition of bodging that he established may one day justify his beatification as the patron saint of Port Isaac's present-day builders and decorators. The name of *Arry Frampton* is already enshrined in the vernacular and his philosophy that to complete a job properly and promptly is of less importance than to spin it out indefinitely by doing as little work on it as can be got away with, provides an everlasting benefit to a grateful village community.

> *"George's box uv day ol' chicks wuz d'liverd s'marnin, en ah zeed George workin' on a run fer a's fowls down be th' bottom uv a's gardin. The way a've 'ung th' ol' wire do look a bit 'Arry Frampton t' me, en ah ken't bleeve a be guyne be aable t'kaype*

many fowls inzide th' bleddy run fer long, that be ef tez ever vineeshed."

Art

All creatures great and small (inclusive of the human species) possess an internal organ known as an *art*. This organ has two defining functions, the most critical of which is to control the healthy circulation of blood to every last corner of the body in which it is hosted. The second function of an *art* is to be taken for granted by its owner and generally ignored until a malfunction takes place. The *art* also features as the subject of far too many popular songs.

> *"Er ordered a gurt jynt uv bayfe fer Zundy dinner, en ah tell ee buhy, twooden aizy t' git ut fer 'er. When 'er come 'long t' th' shop en zeed th' jynt though er zaid twuz too deer fer er pockit, zo 'er dedden want ut. Ah ast 'er what wuz ah guyne do with ut ef er dedden taake ut? Ah tol' 'er, missis ah zayed, ee do ev t' taake un, be Briteesh missis, be Briteesh ah zayed. Er still wooden ev un, en all ah could do wuz ast 'er where wuz er art gone to. Er zayed er dedden want no art fer Zundy dinner nayder."*

With many thanks to Mr J. N. (Boss John) Hicks, Port Isaac Family Butcher

Arve

A broad and substantially heavy item of multi-steel-tined flat-lying farming machinery that is intended to be dragged by either horses or a tractor across recently ploughed fields with the objective of breaking up bigger clods of soil. As with much other farming machinery an *arve* is expensive to purchase and maintain, but please don't worry as anyone who lives in Port Isaac knows that there is no such thing as a poor farmer in St Endellion parish.

"Git yer vit out uv th' way uv that arve buhy! When th' 'oss be pullin' uv un by a dun't never stop fer nobuddy ner nart else."

With many thanks to Mr Mark May of Tregaverne

Arviss

Arviss is the process governing the safe and sure gathering-in of commercial and home grown fruit, cereal, vegetable and general livestock fodder crops at a given point in time, which (weather permitting) normally takes place in the late summer or early autumn of the year. The definitive *arviss* must, by divine decree, be well and truly over "ere the winter storms begin". Curiously enough, whether or not good fortune as measured by crop yield attends the annual *arviss*, both church and chapel invariably stage a service of worship known as an *arviss festyvill* in celebration of success.

"Th' bes' thing 'bout arviss time ez fer we t' git out in the vields when they'm cuttin' th' carn fer 't 'elp th' varmer stook up a's shayves. Tez 'ard nuff work, but there do be s' many bleddy rabbuts runnin' round that us kin alwys be sartin t' caitch 'old uv wan er doo uv em fer t' taake 'ome en hev mother maake a nice pie fer we."

At

An indispensable item of headgear which normally consists of a central crown that can be either soft or rigid—much like the top of the head that it serves to cover—fitted with either a full surround of flat brim or a single forward-jutting peak. The brim (or peak) serves not only to deflect as much rain as is feasible from impinging on the face and/or neck of the *at* wearer, but also to provide a point of reference that one can touch with appropriate servility on encountering one's betters. The most popular variety of *at* seen in Port Isaac is known as a *flattat*. A *flattat* moulds itself to the shape

29

of its owner's head with great panache, and performs the signal duty of absorbing all dirt and grease sent its way, both on the inside and the outside.

> "Ah wooden wear a trilby at ef ah wuz paid t'wear un—a flattat be moo-er proper fer the Likes uv Me. Mind ee, ef zome bugger wuz maazed nuff t' pay ah t' put a trilby on, ah might ev t' think 'bout ut agaane."

Awn

A very useful little word, *awn* finds its place in at least three contexts:

(1) *Awn*—a narrow, cliff-girt rocky cove or inlet opening onto the sea. Depending on its navigability, an *awn* may bear comparison to a harbour. Foreigners tend to use the term "haven" as their preferred alternative to this meaning of *awn*.

(2) *Awn*—a term you might employ in order to claim indisputable personal ownership of something, as in *"Tedden yoo-ers, tez me awn."*

(3) *Awn*—a statement (often made unwillingly) admitting to a misdemeanour you have perpetrated. Thus, *"Ef twuz ee what done ut, ee do better fit awn op."*

> "Mah godfaathers en godmothers, tez a dam good job us got they breakwaters you, 'cuz ah never zeed zays out in th' ol' awn like they ah zeed s'marnin!"

Ay?

(1) *Ay?*—an interrogative device querying the substance of a comment directed at you which you may not have heard in its entirety since as usual you weren't paying much attention at the time.

(2) *Ay?*—a measure of disbelief or scepticism directed at something that you have just been told about.

There are many in Port Isaac who consider an *Ay?* response to be discourteous, but then again if **What?** is used as an alternative it is also reckoned to be rude, so what can a Port Isaac boy do?

"Ay?"
"Straw!
Donkeys ayt ut raw!
Th' moo-er they do ayt,
Th' bigger they do graw!"

"What?"
"Pot!
You'm a fool,
En ah be not!"

A school playground original

Aybenin

The period of the day that occurs between the hours of six and nine o'clock p.m. The *aybenin* is thereby a contrivance aimed at drawing a clear distinction between the afternoon and the night. Its existence simplifies a decision on whether to say "Good evening" or "Good night" would be more appropriate. In the event that the cottage clock has been put forward to summer time, closing off the *aybenin* at ten o'clock p.m. would be acceptable.

"Luv'ly aybenin, you!"
"No tedden you maazed bugger!"

Aych

A means of clarifying at a single stroke the individuality of people or otherwise things of any kind that make up a class, group, gathering, congregation, assembly, collection or what have you. An embarrassing failure to remember Christian names or surnames can then be avoided through the application of **aych**. The word sounds

31

very much like the eighth letter of the alphabet, which as everyone who can recite that far in will know to be spelt *"aich"*. Since with notable exceptions Port Isaac people reject almost all *aiches* at the start of words on sight, the letter sounding like *aych* is of academic interest only.

> *"You bleddy buhys, you'm aych uv ee th' wan s' bad ez th'*
> *tother!"*

Ayge

An elongate construction, typically around six feet in height and up to a yard in width, an *ayge* surrounds and encloses an area of land known as a field. It is built from large stones judiciously piled and fitted the one against the other. The interstices between the stones are packed tight with a mixture of gravel, earth and organic debris. Time generates a covering abundance of wild vegetation which binds the structure together and ensures its longevity. Some of the *ayges* of St Endellion parish may be centuries old. For access to the field which it defines, an *ayge* is normally pierced by one or more strategically located five-bar gates and perhaps a stile or two as well. The field can be directly traversed between opposing *ayges* along what is known as a bridle path—in the improbable event that the farmer who owns the land doesn't object.

> *"Will ee jus' look et th' staate uv un, anybuddy wud think a'd*
> *bin dragged droo a ayge backward!"*

Ayp

A collection of things gathered together which, in the considered opinion of a rational observer, is perceived to numerically comprise rather a lot of items.

> *"Ah wuz down be th' church fer aybenzong, en ah kin tell ee*
> *buhy, there wuz a ole ayp uv paypull en th' congreegaashun.*

Mus' uv bin emmets mos' uv em, zo vicar'll vind a fair foo shillin' in a's colleckshin baags t'night fer shoo-er."

Aypoth

(1) *Aypoth*—a quantity of commercial goods sold for a sum of money equivalent to one four hundred and eightieth of a one pound note. Needless to say, the said quantity of the purchase is probably minuscule, but for the little that it cost who cares?

(2) *Aypoth*—a disparaging categorisation of someone who is assessed by his peers to be a lot less than quick on the uptake.

> *"Kin ah pleeze ev a aypoth of broke biscuits?"*
> *"Sorry buhy, us eb'm got no broke wans."*
> *"Well, kin ee pleeze braake a foo uv em fer me then?"*
> *"Bugger off you daft aypoth afore ah tans yer haass fer ee!"*

Ayster

A major festival of the church calendar. Some say that *Ayster* is the most important festival of them all, although in Port Isaac Christmas gets the popular vote for that honour every time. *Ayster Day* is celebrated on the Sunday following Good Friday, yet in what seems to be one of life's great mysteries, unlike Christmas Day in any given year, neither *Ayster Day* nor Good Friday ever seem to come along on the same calendar dates that they fell on last year. Not that it matters much because on *Ayster Day* the boys and girls get *Ayster aigs* anyway, whatever the date.

> *"Th' bleddy taycher give me such a scat on me aid that ah dedden knaw ef twuz Chrissmuss er Ayster."*

Ayt

Consumption of food by way of mouth. There is no more eagerly anticipated moment in the course of the day in Port Isaac than when a family gathers round the kitchen table and sits down to *ayt* its dinner. Other words used to express the noble tenor of the sentiment imbued in what the act of *aytin* means to Port Isaac boys include *yafflin*, *gobblin*, and *swallerin*. Ensuring that there is enough on the table to *ayt* at set meal times is not only a mother's everlasting concern but also her consuming passion.

> "Git on 'n ayt up whass put in front uv ee buhy, dun't ee knaw there be a war on?"

With many thanks to Mr Jim (Granfer) Creighton of Canadian Terrace

And:

> "Me zister wuz took reel baad las' aybenin. All er could ayt fer brekfiss 'day wuz a drink uv milk."

Ayve

When you have something in your possession of such poor quality that you can't even give it away and which you devoutly wish to be well rid of, your option is to *ayve ut out* somewhere or other, preferably with some forceful momentum behind it. In principle it is possible to *ayve* anything in any direction provided it is not too heavy to tax the strength of the *ayver*. More than a few Port Isaac housewives are reputed to *ayve* items of china at their spouses with considerable accuracy, especially when the latter come home from the "Golden Lion" the worse for drink.

> "Whabbee ah guyne do with all this rubbeesh?
> "Ayve ut out over th' cliff buhy, thass th' bes' way t' git rids uv traade that edden no good!"

Ayzy

A set task that is considered not too difficult to accomplish or fulfil is understood to be *ayzy*. However what is *ayzy* to one person will

34

not necessarily seem *ayzy* to another, thereby making *ayzyniss* a matter for personal judgement and experience.

> *"Oo wuz th' faather uv th' Black Prince?"*
> *"Thass ayzy, twuz ol' King Cole."*

With many thanks to the quick-fire wit of Messrs Bob Monkhouse and Dennis Goodwin

B

Baal

Voiced lamentation expressed with considerable stridency. For no good reason at all that a listener can fathom out, a proper *baal* tends to resound with anguish, rage and (by no means least) petulance consequent on the *baaler*'s perception of having been sorely aggrieved.

> *"You 'ush yer bleddy baal, er ah'll give ee sumthin' proper t' scritch 'bout!"*

Bacca

Not only the revered name of a magnificent botanical species from the kingdom of life-enhancing plants, *bacca* also names the popular commercial product lovingly prepared from the said plant's carefully dried, cured and subsequently finely shredded leaves. This product is savoured by a majority of the general public avid for both its taste and aroma. Some lovers of *bacca* are devoted to its consumption by means of mastication, whereas others favour inhaling a finely powdered variation up into their nostrils. The preponderance of *bacca* users, however, prefer to enclose small quantities of the

36

shredded leaf in a cylinder of paper and thereafter to ignite one end of the cylinder and inhale the ensuing fumes by sucking on the other end. The *bacca* plant was originally native to a warmer clime than that which blesses Port Isaac, yet with local ingenuity, adequate protection from inclemencies of weather and the application of a mulch that owes much to the inclusion of sheep shit, good *bacca* can be successfully cultivated in gardens down in the Port Gaverne valley bottoms.

> *"Paypull be gittin' mayner en mayner—when they ayves 'way fag ends en ee picks em up, ee ken't vind 'ardly any bacca in 'em no moo-er."*

And

> *Bacca do be a aateful weed—*
> *Ah likes ut!*
> *Bacca do be a aateful weed—*
> *Ah likes ut!*
> *Ut maakes ee coff,*
> *Ut maakes ee thin,*
> *Ut do taake th' air*
> *Right off yer chin!*
> *They zay t'smoke ut be a zin.*
> *But ah likes ut!*

With many thanks to the incomparable Mr Ted Robinson of the Harbour Café

Baissly

The consequence of your lack of attention as much to the maintenance of personal hygiene as to the cleanliness of the clothes you wear (all layers inclusive). To come home looking *baissly* is certain to motivate your elders and betters into directing instant outrage at you.

"Will ee jus' lookit yer anns, they'm bleddy baissly! Git on with ee en waish 'em now! Ah wants to' zee proper tidemarks roun' yer risses!"

Balk

A *balk* is a satisfying guttural rumble generated from the base of your throat as intestinally generated gases are forcibly evacuated upwards and outwards through your mouth. The act of *balkin* must not be confused with the related effect of gases which are, with no less a sense of the perpetrator's glee, evicted via the anal orifice to the discomfiture of all who happen to be standing in the immediate vicinity. The best natural *balks* are summoned up at the end of dinner time, but it is left to the lucky exponents of the fine art of air swallowing to produce the most impressive results—such much-envied experts are seemingly able to *balk* at will.

> *Th' maatey's naame wuz Walker—*
> *Mah gar, a wuz a balker!*
> *A could balk anything,*
> *From "God saave the King",*
> *T' 'Arry Frampton's polka!*

With thanks to "'Twas On the Good Ship Venus"—Anon

Be

An irregular verb which provides definitive confirmation of your existence for one and all. Even in Port Isaac any conversation would be incomplete, not to say incomprehensible, without recourse to this very special verb. The declination of its present tense in common Port Isaac usage (and you can't get much more common than that) is as follows:

Positive	Negative
Ah be; Ah are; Ah ez	*Ah ben't; Ah edden*
Ee (or you) be	*Ee ben't; Ee edden*
A (Er) be; A (Er) am	*A (Er) edden*
We be; We am	*We ben't*
You be	*You ben't*
They be; They am	*They ben't; They edden*

"Be ut er ben't ut? Thass th' bleddy kweschin!"

With apologies to Mr William Shakespeare

Belong

Those who *belong* to Port Isaac both enjoy and benefit from the total security of an eternally proud association with this greatest of birthplaces.

> *"Ah do belong t' Port Isaac, but er, she've only lived durty year down ere long with we. Er do belong up the line somewheres, though ah dun't knaw zackly where! Dun't matter reely do ut, cuz they'm all th' zaame up th' line."*

Better fit

The key thrust of a firm suggestion which comes to you mostly from your elders and betters when they observe you to be engaged in the kind of action they consider to be so unconventional that they feel it might be good for the current state of your well being if you were to do things differently.

> *"You baissly bugger you, whaddo ee think you'm doin' uv? Tez Zundy! Better fit ee wuz down church with they other buggers zingin bleddy 'ims!"*

39

Bile

A phenomenon associated with precipitate bubbling and the generation of steam which takes place when a quantity of water placed in a receptacle is incrementally heated up to a temperature of either one hundred degrees Centigrade or two hundred and twelve degrees Fahrenheit. If water is not allowed to *bile*, its use in the preparation of tea is rendered impracticable.

> *"You'm guyne ev t' wait fer yer dish uv tay, th' kittle wun't bile till th' ol' vire gits drawed up a bit."*

Beshap

Beshap is a most-reverend ranking title awarded to only a select number of clergymen by the Church hierarchy. Both the personage of the *beshap* and the mystique of his office are held in awe by Port Isaac churchgoers. The *beshap* of Cornwall, whose region of responsibility (technically known as a *dyasis* yet referred to rather more evocatively where the boys are concerned as a *beshap prick*) includes St Endellion parish, is based at the cathedral down in Truro and seldom flashes his mitre in the wild north of the county.

> *"'Ere buhy, you goes t' church, ev ee ever zeed th' beshap?"*
> *"S' far ez ah do knaw, zince a dun't much layve Troora, and ah dun't never go down along there, ah ebben zeed un. We maakes do with prayin' fer th' bugger in church every Zundy though."*

Blab

The unsolicited transfer of gratuitous (and for the most part unverifiable) information and (better yet) rumours by word of mouth in the streets. The measure of success of an expert *blab* in Port Isaac is considered to be directly proportional not only to its vindictive content but also to the speed by which it gets disseminated throughout the community to the detriment of its subject.

> *"Dun't ee tell er nart buhy, tez knawn that er do always blab er bleddy aid off t' ooever er maytes."*

In fond memory of Miss Mary Bate of Rat's Terrace, lower Front Hill

Bleddy

This is one of the most useful words in the whole Port Isaac lexicon. *Bleddy* is an adjective for all seasons. It can be linked to almost any imaginable noun. It totally eliminates the tiresome demands of the teachers for you to develop a vocabulary. Why should you have to search for an adjective when *bleddy* is always there to fit the bill? As Humpty Dumpty might have put it, when this good word is used it means just what it is chosen to mean—neither more nor less.

> *"Th' bleddy weather do be s' bad, ah ken't git th' bleddy boat out droo th' bleddy awn, en with all th' grownzay us be evin' ah knaws that when ah kin git out en ah pulls me bleddy pots there edden guyne be bugger all in em."*

Bleeve

This is what you aver by rote when you recite the Apostles' Creed. Whether you mean it or not is quite another matter of course.

> *"Th' bleddy council in Waybridge do promise th' Likes uv We in Port Isaac s' much en d' do s' little fer we that ah tell ee buhy ah dun't knaw what t' bleeve 'bout em."*

Bollicks

A *bollick* is no less, and certainly no more, than a single testicle. Generally speaking, nearly every Port Isaac man (and boy) possesses a pair of the same, hence it is customary to speak of *bollicks* in the plural. Incidentally, *bollicks* also refers to the tenor of the majority of opinions expressed by most Port Isaac fishermen and all politicians.

> *Bollicks! En th' zaame t' you!*
> *Bollicks! En ee kin clayne 'em too!*
> *Bollicks! When ah zays bollicks,*
> *Then ah maynes bollicks, jus' bollicks, t' you!*
>
> *'Itler, a only 'ad wan ball.*
> *Goerin' 'ad two, but they wuz small.*
> *'Immler wuz very zim'lar,*
> *But Goebels 'ad no balls atall!*
>
> *Bollicks! En th' zaame t' you!*
> *Bollicks! En ee kin clayne 'em too!*
> *Bollicks! When ah zays bollicks,*
> *Then ah maynes bollicks, jus' bollicks, t' you!*

With thanks to the Colonel Bogey march and an anonymous lyricist (praise be on him).

Bommin

A first-time visitor to the Cornish town named *Bommin* will probably find himself doing a double-take on two counts. The first count will be motivated by the town's unremittingly bleak aspect, and the second will be accompanied with incredulity when the visitor is amazed to learn that he is standing in the capital of Cornwall. This mean place is feared throughout the county thanks to the presence of a great grim-walled lunatic asylum on its outskirts. In the public consciousness the characteristics of insanity and the name *Bommin* are virtually synonymous. As to why *Bommin* was allowed to assume capital status when Truro (where the county's sole cathedral is located) would appear to be more eminently qualified, and since in any case alternative candidates with a far more aesthetically pleasing aspect could easily be found, there is no good answer. Down at the school in Port Isaac the teachers are apt to advise their pupils at the drop of a blot that Cornwall has (or had) three options for its capital town—Truro because it ought to be, Launceston because it used to be, and *Bommin* because it is. So much for that.

"Th' way ee do be'aave, you'm s' maazed ez a brish. Ee do belong in Bommin!"

With thanks to Mr Michael "Cogs" Collings of the Old Coastguard Station

Bones

When you are *on yer bones* you find yourself living in a state of impecuniousness to which one or more of the following symptoms is applicable—(a) there is an empty fag packet in your pocket and having the next smoke is long overdue; (b) there is an absence of the wherewithal within your pockets to purchase even a meagre half pint of Walter Hicks' piss up at the Golden Lion; (c) you lack a couple of bob to wager on a hot tip that a particular gee gee is a dead cert to win; and (d) when the collection bag comes to you in church you have to put an empty hand into it and surreptitiously tap the bag with the other hand to make it clink and give an impression to the church warden that you have contributed your dues.

"Where did that bugger git they noo boots? A's normal on th' bones of a's haass, without doo coppers t' rub t'gither. A mus' uv whipped uv 'em in Waybridge when the shopkeeper's back wuz turned!"

Bottoms

The *bottoms* are well-established valley floors on which streamlets meander, marshy conditions predominate and where hither and thither deposits of rich black silt support a riot of luxuriant weeds. The Port Isaac and Port Gaverne valley *bottoms* are excellent examples of this. It would be remiss not to mention the Port Quin

43

bottoms as well. Black *bottoms* silt can be tamed and tilled to liberate orderly gardens where vegetables and (hopefully) *bacca* supplant weeds and go on to luxuriate and thrive until they are harvested.

> *"Ah likes bein' up in th' bottoms bes' when all they yella irises comes out en th' withies starts grawin' long."*

Boss-eyed

An astigmatic condition which causes the pupil of an afflicted subject's left eye to be permanently focussed well to the right of centre, and/or alternatively the pupil of the subject's right eye to be focussed equally well to the left of centre. Anyone with a "normally" focussed pair of eyes can, through energetic trial and error, endeavour to achieve a momentary playground-pleasing *boss-eyed* look. Practitioners of the art are forcibly advised by their elders and betters that should the wind change while their eyes are *bossed*, the *bossing* will be irreversible.

> *"Er wuz s' boss-eyed er could zee when er needed to git on en dig chuggy pigs out uv 'er nose."*

Boughten

A qualification applied to any item of retail goods that you purchase from a vendor in exchange for the precise tally of coins (or notes) of the realm that the vendor demands of you. When edible merchandise of the kind that you would expect to be either prepared at home or dug up out of the back garden is *boughten*, the product quality is understood to be of an inferior nature.

> *"Ah dun't go much on that bleddy zaffern caake. It do fall abroad when ee dips un en yer tay. Course, tez boughten, s' what else kin ee speck?"*

Braake

A declivitous sheltered hollow nestling in the side of a valley. Not infrequently wooded to the point of being impenetrable, a *braake* drains directly down slope to the valley *bottoms*.

> "*If you'm lookin' t' git a maggie's aig, ah knaws be a cupple maggie nests up in Skarrick braake, but ah do tell ee, tez awful ard t' git yer and into th' nest droo all they blackthorns.*"

Braave

A ubiquitous adjective used to specify all things superlative. Something described as being *braave* will, for good or ill, be certain to have mightily impressed the perception of he who made the observation.

> "*Ef ee wuz t' go down be th' baych ee'd zee zich braave zays rollin' en! Put on yer ileskins mind ee, th' bleddy wind do be s' braave en cold that when a blaws th' spray at ee t'will taake th' whiskers off yer faace.*"

Braid

The quintessential product of the baker's craft, *braid* is prepared from a well-loved set of tried and true ingredients in which flour, water, yeast and salt are all writ large. These ingredients are skilfully mixed to form a dough which, when sufficient time has elapsed to allow the constituent parts to get used to one another, is further kneaded, appropriately subdivided, shaped and placed in an oven to be baked for an allotted period of time. The final outcome is known as a *lowfabraid* and features a crusty exterior enclosing a soft and sensual interior—characteristics that some (but not many) denizens of the Port Isaac Town Platt may be said to share. The *Likes uv They* typically trim off and dispose of the crusts so as to consume only the soft part of the *braid,* whereas the *Likes uv We* always eat the lot, crusts and all, right down to the last stale crumb.

> *"Ere, passon in a's zermon las' aybenzong tol' we that man ken't live be braid alone. Tez awright fer he—that bugger kin afford butter t' put on a's braid s' well ez jam, while th' bes th' Likes uv We kin do is t' try en vind a bit uv drippin' fer spraidin'."*

In appreciation of Sherratt's Bakery of lower Fore Street

Brish

A very common household implement consisting of a flat wooden headpiece embellished on one side with an ingenious geometrical arrangement of bristles and precariously attached on the other side to a long wooden handle. The ready intricacy of the formation of bristles has led to the humble *brish* being used as a metaphor for erratic (*maazed*) human behaviour. When the handle of a *brish* is agitated with a to and fro motion known as *swaypin,* the bristles, provided they are not worn away too much, are instrumental in moving the dirt and other debris lying on the floor both inside and outside of a cottage from one place to another.

> *"Faather, th' ol' cat ev brought in a daid rat."*
> *"Well, whaddo ee want me t' do maid? Git'old uv th' brish en swaype un out th' doo-er fer zum other bugger t' pick up!"*

Britches

Underwear designed to clad the female form between the waist and the knees. Some types of *britches* are rather more voluminous than others. *Britches* are manufactured from a variety of textiles, the textures of which range all the way from sackcloth thickness to a fineness verging on virtual non-existence. A common characteristic of all *britches* is elastication around both the waist and the holes that the legs go through—elastic is famous for losing its tension at the most inappropriate moments, as described in the celebrated book *Coming Down* by Lucy Lastic. An alternative name for **britches** is **nickers**—the latter being beloved of Port Isaac playground poets since it rhymes so well with "vicars."

> *"Ah come pas' ol' mother Hambly's plaace s'marnin, en er 'ad er waishin' out on th' bleddy line with zeverl pair uv britches fair t' zee, billering out in the wind s'if er wuz still in em."*

And moreover:

> *Whass th' time?*
> *Appass nine!*
> *Ang yer britches*
> *On th' line!*

In fond memory of Mr Nicholas Hicks of New Road

Broad

A measure of the degree of obscurity in which the tones of conversational English are cloaked (and even totally disguised) by virtue of local accent. A **broad** accent stamps the hallmark of identity. Even if they wanted to, which they don't, the people of Port Isaac are unable to hide just how **broad** their accent is.

> *"Ah maade th' mistaake uv stoppin off in th' ol' "Bettle en Chisel" up be Dellybole las' wayke, en ah do tell ee, th' way they buggers spaykes up there do be s' broad en s' deffernt t' th' way we spaykes in Port that me ears dedden knaw ef they wuz comin er guyne."*

Bugger

Bugger is a universally popular all-purpose noun with an inherent power and vitality drawn right out of the contextual stable of that universal adjective *bleddy.* Together with bleddy, this magnificent word is not infrequently used to hone a double-edged sword suitable for gracing any verbal duel. With appropriate support, *bugger* is guaranteed to provide the ardent conversationalist with a satisfyingly accurate means of describing practically anything, whether it happens to be of animal (with particular relevance to males of the species *Homo sapiens*), vegetable, mineral or abstract derivation. Females tend to be excluded from being referred to as *buggers*, although it is more than likely that most Port Isaac males would be acquainted with a few females who would more than adequately justify being given the title.

"Tez a reel bugger sloggin' up t' Endellion over that ol' path droo they bleddy vields."

"Dun't ah knaw et buhy, though ah do think th' proper bugger uv ut do be that th' varmer oo's land tez ez zich a miser'ble ol' bugger. A dun't look aafter th' path. Ee do ev t' waitch out fer un!"

"Aiz buhy, but a's cheel Bill edden zich a baad bugger atall. Coorse ah knawed he since a wuz a little tacker down be th' bleddy skool."

In appreciation of Mr Joe Dawe of Pennant Farm

And from Sunday school:

"It was reported to me that you boys have been heard using bad language in the streets! Now I don't wan't to hear about this sort of thing again!"

"Well then zur, tez bes' ef ee dun't lissen t' they oo tells ee no bleddy moo-er! Whabbee us t' zay then ef us gits maazed with zumwan?"

"Well, when I get annoyed I just say, oh pish."

"Git on with ee zur, tez a ole ayp better t' zay bugger ut!"

In fond memory of Mr Tim Scawin of Rose Hill

Buhy

A favoured means of personal address which falls as music on the ears of males of all ages. Being called *buhy* invests you with a high degree of subjective affection. Age not only presents no barrier to the appellation of *buhy* but revels in the accolade. The female equivalent of this great and glorious title is *maid*, yet while *ol' buhy* is always acceptable to the ears, *ol' maid* is most decidedly not.

> *"Git on with ee buhy! Ow be ee? You'm lookin' braave en wisht!"*
>
> *"Well buhy, ah s'pose ah 'ev fayled a bit, but bugger me, ah ken't speck much else now ah be near on aady cep' fer a wan way ticket up t' Endellion!"*

C

Caake

Another excellent product of the baker's craft, as many types of *caake* are traditionally baked at home as are made commercially available to the public in *boughten* form. A fair few of the ingredients used to make *braid* are also applicable to *caake*—additions in the latter instance consisting of items such as eggs, milk, sugar, saffron, caraway seeds, nuts, currants and sultanas. A typical *caake* has a round shape, matching the standard form of the tin in which it was baked. Decorations which both garnish and enhance the appearance of the top of a *caake* include *marzeepan*, white or cocoa-coloured *eyesin*, *jaam*, *hunderds en thousinds* and (perish the thought) *flemmunturd*. The most common varieties of *caake* eaten in Port Isaac are *zaffern*, *yaiss*, *spunje*, *Crissmuss*, *birfdy* and *zeed*, which is not to imply that any or all of them are popular with everyone, especially where *zeed* is concerned.

> "*Ere, will ee ev a slice uv caake?*"
> "*Oo maade un?*"
> "*Maade un mezelf!*"
> "*No thanks then maid, me Gran tol' me never t' ayt nart*

that come out uv yoo-er oven."

In loving memory of Mrs Eleanor (Gran) Creighton of Canadian Terrace

Cafflick

A *cafflick* is a devotee of a fundamental religious movement headed up by a garishly dressed high priest bearing the title of "Pope". That gentleman's remote grasp of the realities of life as lived by the *Likes uv We* is manifested in (a) the ostentation of his residence and associated retinue at an opulent palace located in the heart of Rome; (b) his insistence on conducting much of his business in Latin, (c) his outright eschewing of the institution of marriage not only for himself but also for his priestly acolytes; and (d) the hierarchy of self-righteous predators who feed on the more vulnerable of his followers. *Cafflicks* are to all intents and purposes either thin on the ground or non-existent in Port Isaac—a circumstance looked on with approbation by all residents of the village who owe their allegiance to Church and Chapel. In their historical heyday *Cafflicks* were forever seeking world dominion through waging wars, conducting savage inquisitions of all who disagreed with their point of view which featured prolonged torture, burning at the stake, condemnation to hell and so on and so forth. Port Isaac doesn't want any of that thank you.

> *"Johnny, what is wrong with this sentence—the priest slipped on the altar steps and hurted his knee?"*
>
> *"Dun't knaw miss, ah be chapel! Ah ben't no cafflick, but s'far ez ah do be consarned, ef a urted a's laig ut do sarve th' bugger right fer not lookin' where a wuz guyne."*

With thanks to Mr H. Allen Smith, noble humorist

Cahrr

The practical means by which something whether animate or

inanimate is borne from one place to another either by one person acting on his own or a number of people co-operating in concert. A word of warning to the wise—whatever you are required to *cahrr* should not be so heavy as to over-tax your ability to *cahrr* it.

> "*Ez a strong? Ah do tell ee, that bugger kin cahrr a sack uv tetties on aych uv a's shoulders frum ere to Port Quin en never ev t' stop be th' ayge fer a piss moo-er'n wance!*"

Canvas

A commodity to cover and thereby improve the appearance of a domestic floor, *canvas* is manufactured in great sheets decorated in a choice of colours and patterns substantial enough to suit even the most jaundiced of tastes, and sold to the public in great rolls. It is much used by the many Port Isaac cottage dwellers who cannot afford proper carpeting on their cottage floors. *Canvas* has a glossy upper surface which appears to be designed to ensure that sooner or later anyone who walks on it habitually is going to slip and fall over. A more critical property of *canvas* is its ability to retain a coldness of particular intensity, as the touch on it in the night of a bare foot fresh from a warm bed when nature calls will bear witness.

> "*Mother, there do be a 'ole in th' floo-er 'longzide th' mangle in th' waish 'ouse!*"
> "*Dun't ee worry maid, jus'do ee shove a bit uv canvas over un en maake shoo-er ee dun't step on un after!*"

Cap'n

An honorary title much in vogue as a means of address from one good-old-bugger type to another, *Cap'n* demonstrates a high level of respect enveloped in much affection.

> "*Ow be ee, Cap'n?*"
> "*Ah edden s' bad Cap'n, en tomorra ef ah waakes up en*"

edden daid ah specks t'will be the zaame then too buhy!"

In fond memory of Mr Leonard "Cockeye" Mitchell of Hartland Road

Carkin

An overt act of intrusion, typically in the commission of which an habitual loser inveigles himself into the proximal company of others who seem to be enjoying some success, in the evident anticipation that at least some of their good fortune will rub off on him. *Carkin* is carried out as if the gathering of proverbial crumbs from the table of the *Likes uv They* are no more than the *carker's* due on the road to turning around a persistent lack of luck through touching the hem of fortune's cloak.

> *"When th' ol' **Maple Leaf** wuz out off Varley Aid catchin' stones uv mackerl with th' lines comin' up vull ever' time, ah zeed the bleddy **Lilla** carkin' uv 'er right up longzide en gittin' 'ardly a vish fer ut, zo zerve the bugger right!"*

In appreciation of Messrs Anthony Provis of the Old Council Houses and Bill "Pink" Brown of Rose Hill.

Carn

The basic commercial cereal crop husbanded by farmers in the hinterland of Port Isaac Bay. *Carn* consists of an equal mix of oats and barley, allegedly sown together on the principle that if the oats fail to prosper due to the weather being too dry then the barley which favours wetter conditions should thrive—naturally enough vice-versa is applicable. The final *carn* harvest ought to guarantee the least of both worlds, but you can't tell a Port Isaac farmer that. For that matter you can't tell a Port Isaac farmer very much at all.

> *"When th' carn be 'igh us loves t' coose droo ut en veel th' stalks en aids uv th' barley swishin' long be our laigs."*

Carner

The blunt point of sealed pastry at either of the two lateral terminations of a pasty are the pasty's *carners*. A *carner* is formed when the pasty cook brings together the edges of the pastry base over the pasty contents and subjects them to an expert twisting technique known in the trade as *crimpin*. The anatomy of a pasty comprises two *carners* separated by a *middle*. The *carners* are key repositories of delectable gravy generated within the pasty during the baking process. Pastiophiles reckon that the liquid volume of gravy residing in *carners* is directly proportional to the skill of the pasty cook. It should be noted in passing that any attribution of the pasty synonym *tetty oggie* to a Cornish origin is incorrect—Devon is to blame for that particular offence.

> *"They do zay that Missis Sherratt kin ayt a apple without putting en er valse teef, but ah bet ee that ayben she cudden bite droo a carner uv wan uv Win Brown's pasties, en ah speck a lopster would vind Win's carners ard nuff guyne too you."*

In appreciation of Miss Winifred "Winnie" Brown of upper Fore Street

Caw!

An expletive that you can utter in mixed company without your having to fear that anyone present will turn an eyeball, let alone a hair. When you say "*Caw!*" you are implying that whatever you have just seen at first hand wouldn't have been considered credible had it been passed onto you as mere hearsay. Acceptable alternatives to *caw!* are found in the expression *mah godfathers en godmothers!* Or, putting it more simply yet, in *well ah'll be buggered!*

> *"Caw! ef ah edden zeed ut with me own eyes 'ow many scoo-ers uv thousinds uv errins wuz shook out uv th' nets s'marnin ah would uv called any bugger oo tole me bout ut a bleddy liard!"*

Cawl

A substance that would be definitively classified as "mineral" if announced by Eamonn Andrews as the next object for Norman Hackforth to tell listeners (but not the panel) about in "Twenty Questions". Black and dusty in appearance, *cawl* is a naturally occurring fuel that occurs underground and is obtained from mines. Destined for use in the cottage fireplace, *cawl* is delivered to domestic premises in sacked-up one hundred and twelve pound lots known as *hunderds* by a grimy gentleman, caped and aproned in worn leather and referred to as the *cawlman*.

> *Ol' King Cawl*
> *Wuz a merry ol' sawl,*
> *En a merry ol' sawl t' zee.*
> *A olled fer a light en th' middle uv th' night,*
> *Guyne off t' th' lavatree.*
> *Th' moon wuz shinin' on th' lavatree doo-er,*
> *Th' candle 'ad a frite,*
> *Ole King Cawl*
> *Valled down th' ole*
> *En comed up cover'd in shite.*

In fond memory of Mr Harold Spry, coalman of Trewetha Lane and the Terrace

Chacks

Any fleshy and vulnerable part of a boy or girl's body which his or her elders and betters consider to offer an attractive target for the administration of corporal punishment by way of hand.

> *"Ah zeed that buhy paraadin long th' ayge uv th' cliff down be Port Gaverne, en ef a belonged t' me when a comed 'ome en ah could git old uv un ah'd a giv'd un a good smack round th' chacks fer doin uv ut."*

With thanks to Mrs Dorothy "Dar" Williams of Hartland Road

Chapel

The categorisation of all Port Isaac residents whose religious affiliation is devoted to an evangelistic movement reputedly started up by Mr John Wesley and his colleagues a couple of centuries ago. Method is mandatory in shaping the *Chapel* allegiance. In sharp contrast to their sworn arch-rivals of the *Church*, *Chapel* people favour less formality in services of worship and have little tolerance for the great range of arcane trappings in which *Church* goers place such great store. *Chapel* people are additionally distinguished by being frequently preached at by semi-articulate local amateurs, in their enjoyment of rousing hymns, through the maintenance in the anonymity of their own homes of a quantity of strong drink to be taken strictly for medicinal purposes, and for their abhorrence of visiting places of entertainment (including public houses) whenever and wherever there is a risk that they may be recognised on the premises.

> *"Th' way a do talk, that local praychur do think that zunshine do come out uv a's haass. A's proper chapel frum aid t' vit, but a's guyne end up in th' ground up be Endellion saame as all uv we be, so us ben't all that differnt frum un reely."*

In fond memory of Messrs Wesley Blake of Front Hill and Harold Provis of the Old Council Houses

Chaw

A *chaw* is an approximately half-inch long piece of specially processed *bacca* that has been surgically excised from one end of a thin rope-like coil of the same with the assistance of a clasp knife and a calloused thumb. The coil of *bacca* resembles a stick of liquorice crossed with a heavily tarred twist of binder twine. Once cut, a *chaw* is transferred to the mouth of the *bacca chawer* with a dexterity that only experience can guarantee. Within the safe haven of the mouth the chaw is rhythmically masticated with a demonstration of pleasure that may be more forced than genuine. Under the thrall of champing teeth (natural or false) a *chaw* (sometimes referred to as a *quid* and happily costing only a fraction of that monetary namesake with which most Port Isaac pockets have little familiarity) is certain to generate substantial volumes of rank expectorant which the *chawer* will discharge not only unexpectedly but also with an impressive lack of concern as to where it ends up. In an action known as *quidding* an expert can remove a *chaw* from his mouth with one sweep of a forefinger and proceed in an instant to shove it into a boy's mouth for the unalloyed joy of appreciating the boy's discomfiture. A boy once *quidded* will be rather more than twice shy of approaching a *chawer* in future.

> *"Tez bes' t' kaype clear uv th' bleddy vishermen when they'm zittin yarnin en evin a chaw. They'm s' like t' spit on a buhy ez not! En ee speshly got t' look out fer ol' Jack Shite when a do 'ev a chaw in—that miserble ol' bugger kin spit en scat a flay from dree yard off!"*

In appreciation of the great character actor and comedian Mr Bernard Miles

Cheldern

All members of the Port Isaac community in an age range from birth up to when they leave school to start a full-time job of work, are *cheldern*. The singular of *cheldern* is *cheel*. The everyday conduct of *cheldern's* lives is subject to the mixed blessing of their being wholly subservient to the dictates of their parents, elders and betters, with regard to whom they are expected to be seen but not heard.

> *"Where be all th' cheldern to, mother?"*
> *"They'm all out zumwheres, though ah dun't reely knaw*

zackly where they'm to. Still, never do ee mind, when dinner time do come ee'll zee uv um zoonnuff."

Chimbly

A vertical to sub-vertical hollow conduit built within the wall of a cottage in order to link a fireplace with the freedom of the four winds up at rooftop level. The twin attributes of a *chimbly* are (a) to ensure that as much fire-generated smoke as possible is evacuated up into the open air despite all the efforts of the prevailing wind to blow much of it back down again, and (b) to form a repository in which a lot of soot can accumulate and go on to cause great excitement when it eventually catches fire. According to conventional wisdom, an umbrella will easily go up a *chimbly* when it is down, yet once it has emerged at the top it will defy all efforts to compel it to go back down again when it is up.

> *"Ef ee dun't zee no smoke comin out uv 'er chimbly tez possible er've gone 'way, but moo-er likely t'will be that er's daid cuz er do never let th' ol' vire go out when er do be 'ome."*

Chuggy-pig

A solid chunk of nasal discharge combining both style and substance with the velocity of a projectile. A typical *chuggy-pig* is equipped with a hard crust at its downstream end and a tendency to be mostly green in colour and increasingly sloppy in texture in the upstream direction.

> *"All they cheldern frum up Wetha way, they comes down t' school moo-er often'n not with chuggy pigs angin' out uv their noses, but t' give 'em zome doos, when the taychur do tell em uv ut they wipes ut off on their coat slayves."*

Church

Those who are *Church* are the antitheses—some would say the nemeses—of those who are *Chapel* and vice versa. The rift dividing these religious predilections is as severe and as deep as the Gut which separates the Port Gaverne Main from Castle Rock. *Church* people are nothing if not clannish. *Church* is actually short for *Churchuvinglind* which even the bishop down in Truro must reckon to be a bit of a mouthful. In both secular and religious modes all that is *Church* in Port Isaac moves in accordance with the wiles and whims of the vicar. On the credit side however, although *Church* and *Chapel* people exhibit a poorly disguised disdain for one another, their relationship has much of a love–hate quality about it and they all prefer to direct most of their factional distaste towards a loathing for *Cafflicks*.

> "*Tez funny you, ah do go t' Zundy skool down be church every Zundy af'noon en do aate ut, but when ut do come t' th' Zundy skool Chrissmuss party ah edden s' zorry that ah put me time en droo th' year t' git in on that biggest bleddy faist uv th' 'ole Church callinder.*"

In fond memory of the Reverend W. Atterbury Thomas of the Vicarage

And yet,

> *Wherever ee do be,*
> *Let yer wind braake free!*
> *Fer 'oldin th' wind*
> *Wuz th' death uv me!*
> *In church er chapel,*
> *Let ut rattle!*

Allegedly carved on a tombstone somewhere or other in Cornwall.

59

Cloze

A sack (sometimes literally) term describing the apparel that you clad your body with, especially when you are required to expose yourself to the critical gaze of the general public. Most *cloze* seen on the people of Port Isaac are likely to be characterised by a high frequency of darning and/or patching at the elbows, knees, backside and heels where they are most subject to self-imposed wear and tear. When a grubbiness that can no longer be ignored has attached itself to *cloze*, washing the *cloze* is normally the order of the day. It is no secret that Port Isaac men favour wearing *cloze* distinguished by various shades of black in order to mask the presence of dirt. The so-called *bess* sets of *cloze* are kept in the presence of mothballs in cupboards, from where they are taken out only to make an ostentatious display on Sundays and at funerals.

> *"Ol' Andra Mitchell tol' me that a dun't mind atall that a's wife Vera ev got s' much cloze in 'er cubberts. Andra zaid that th' better er do dress, th' pleasder a do be."*

In fond memory of Mr Andrew Mitchell of Hartland Road

Collinder

A kitchen utensil made of enamelled metal, a *collinder* has the overall shape of a round dish, deep enough when turned upside down to make a cover for your head. A *collinder* has a pair of diametrically opposed hoop-like handles riveted onto its upper rim and is intensely perforated all over with small circular holes grouped in vaguely pleasing patterns. Its key function is to receive and drain over-cooked vegetables tipped straight out of the saucepan in which their trial by boiling was carried out.

> *"A dun't never knaw what t' do with azelf when tez baad weather outzide. A's like a fart in a collinder, chargin' round en round en not knawin' which 'ole to git out uv fust."*

(It is generally considered perfectly acceptable to substitute *"blue-haassed fly"* for *"fart in a collinder"* under normal circumstances.)

Coortin

An intimate relationship between an alleged bachelor and an alleged spinster of the parish incorporating psychological and social imperatives which appear to afflict the pair of them simultaneously. Anyone with the rumour-monger's eye for spotting a *coortin cupple* will not only initiate a whispering campaign focussed on a burgeoning romance but is also likely to suggest an eventual marriage (subject to the couple being of age) in the offing. On each and every Sunday the *News of the World* newspaper provides its many readers in Port Isaac with thinly veiled reports implying that *coortin* is not only an activity sometimes practised by same-sex couples but one that also involves extra-marital romps involving actresses and bishops in which intimacy invariably occurs. Although such goings on tend to be frowned upon in the gossip centres of Port Isaac, they are undoubtedly read and thought about with extraordinary avidity in the privacy of the cottage home.

> *"When ah went off gulls-aigin' up t' Bounds cliff t'other aybenin ah nearby valled over a coortin couple in th' long graass when ah come climbin over th' ayge. Ah ad t' coose off s' fast ez ah could, en ah do tell ee ah pretty near shitted mezelf s'much ez they pair mustuv did et th' zaame time!"*

Coose

A repetitively rapid to-and-fro movement of your feet performed either when you want to pursue someone you are keen to lay your hands on or otherwise to ensure a timely escape from the clutches of someone who is equally anxious to catch you. Success devolves on he who can *coose* the faster.

"*Th' varmer 'oo awns th' archurd down be Port Quin valley come 'long while we wuz scrumpin' uv a's apples. Us dedden zee un comin', en the bugger coosed we neerly all th' way up t' Long Cross afore a gived up.*"

Copper

There are two distinctive meanings to this word:

(1) *Copper*—a term applicable to each of the three coins of the realm (namely the farthing, the ha'penny and the penny) which are usually dull brown in colour when they emerge from your pocket. By contrast, in their newly minted condition the same coins are always shiny, reflecting the pristine colour of the metal with the chemical symbol Cu and atomic weight of 65.54 that they are made from.

"*Gypsy Crocker come t' our doo-er las' Zatdy zellin' cloze-paigs. Er wanted zilver in er ann, but all ah ad en me purse t' give er wuz a foo coppers, en that maade she maazed nuff t' put a curse on me aid!*"

(2) *Copper*—a labour-saving device which comes into service on washing day (Monday, when else?) A *copper* consists of a large font-like hemispherical cast iron bowl built into the top of an approximately four feet high open-fronted brick construction within the base of which a fire can be laid and ignited. The cast iron bowl is initially half filled with cold water for subsequent heating by the fire to a temperature suitable for dropping in clothes to be washed in association with some soap and a muslin-bound fragment of Reckitt's Blue. A domestic *copper* is normally located in a small room, shed or outhouse named the *waishhouse*. Handy accessories for a *copper* include a mangle in its near vicinity, a rope line set up and ready in the back garden, and a selection of Gypsy Crocker's wooden clothes pegs in a chip basket well to hand.

"*Wance th' waishin be done, we likes t' put tetties in the raid 'ot cawls under th' ol' copper, baake uv em till they'm black skinned, then ayt em fer our dinner."*

Countin'

Countin is a fundamental feature of the third of the three "R's" as they are taught down at the Port Isaac County Primary School. Some Port Isaac boys even get to master it in time. *Countin* requires numbers to be marshalled in order; memorised; and used to tally up various things of both manufactured and natural origin. Whether the things are alive or dead is immaterial to the *countin* process. The greatest heights of *countin* achievement seen in Port Isaac are scaled by men working out the returns for a winning accumulator on a race card or alternatively keeping a running darts or billiards score or maybe even doing both at the same time. It would be rare indeed for a Port Isaac man, whether numerate or innumerate, to permit himself to be short-changed.

The basic order of the numbers from one to twenty as used in *countin* is as follows:

> *wan, doo, dree, vower, vahve, zecks, zeb'm, aate, nahn, den, leb'm, dwelve, dirteen, farteen, viffdeen, zecksdeen, zeb'mdeen, aadeen, nahndeen, dwenny.*

Thereafter the sequence runs *dwenny wan, dwenny doo, dwenny dree* … all the way up to *dwenny nahn* and *dirty* and so on through *farty, viffdy, zecksdy, zeb'mdy, aady, nahndy* and *hunderd*.

It is worth pointing out that the sequence of numbers continues onwards and ever-onwards well beyond a *hunderd*, although moving too far ahead of that huge number brings with it an increasing demand for concentration that feels too much like hard work for a Port Isaac boy to worry about in the here and now. For the sake of purists it can be herewith put on record that the number "eleventy" does not exist.

63

"Ow much longer be ee guyne taake—ee mus' uv vineeshed th' zum that ah gived ee be now?"

"Aiz miss, ah 'ev vineeshed un. Ah bin countin uv un vahve times, en ere's me vahve differnt ansers!"

In appreciation of the Port Isaac County Primary School infants class teacher Miss Smythe

Crame

A magnificent component of fresh Cornish milk removed only recently from the udder of a Cornish cow, *crame* is hailed by those who know it well as a foodstuff far more supreme in divine quality than manna and ambrosia combined. *Crame* is famed far and wide beyond the borders of the delectable duchy of Cornwall as a quintessential element of Cornish cuisine. In order to prepare *crame* the fresh (or *raw*) milk is allowed to stand for a few hours in a large enamel basin prior to being placed (in the same basin) over a source of modest heat on which it is "scalded" up to a temperature just short of boiling point. The basin is then removed from the heat and set on one side to cool—during the cooling *crame* rises to the surface of the scalded milk where it gathers as if by magic in golden-yellow clotted rafts. The accumulated *crame* can then be scooped out with a big spoon for transfer to a basin. *Crame* is often used to enhance the appeal of jellies, blancmanges and trifles, but finds its most important role as a topping on splitters that have been spread with a thick layer of jam or treacle. The use of butter or margarine in combination with *crame* is a culpable offence. Treacle covered with *crame* is sometimes referred to as *thundernlightnin*.

"Tez zum vunny t' zee they emmets evin' their tay downtown be th' Arbour caffy! They do put crame on the splitters fust en jaam on top uv that! They'm zum ancient you!"

In fond memory of Mr Hillson and his son Horace of Hillson's Farm

Crimp

The braided seal of pastry which ideally sweeps in an open, slightly off-centre curve from corner to corner on top of a proper pasty. The elegance of a well-wrought *crimp* is not only directly related to its maker's skill, it also confirms the identity of the maker as effectively as would the maker's handwritten signature (always assuming of course that the said pasty maker can write).

> *"Ah loves paasties, but ah ken't alwys old with all that paastry guyne inta th' crimps, speshly in boughten wans where ee do mostly git moo-er paastry than innerds. Ah puts they sort uv crimps in me trowsis pocket when Gran edden lookin', then ah ayves 'em out on th' ol' baych fer th' gulls t' fight over laater on."*

Crissmuss

It is the universal belief of the god-fearing and the good people of Port Isaac that the period established around *Crissmuss Day* makes the very best time of the whole year. *Crissmuss Day* always falls on the twenty-fifth of December and, in celebration of its glory, impressively cheap gifts are traditionally exchanged by family members to the secret dismay of all recipients. Widely recognised as an occasion for family celebration however, the season of *Crissmuss* includes several initial weeks of growing anticipation during which the remaining number of available shopping days prior to the event is regularly announced in the newspapers as well as on the wireless. *Crissmuss Day* itself is sooner or later pretty much guaranteed to generate a degree of disharmony between family members of an even more conflictive kind than that which prevails during the rest of the year. On the other hand a good row has never done any lasting harm to anyone in Port Isaac. Striking a more positive note on *Crissmuss Day*, **Crissmuss** carols are sung around the dinner table communally if tunelessly, and with a bit of luck there may be a roasted chicken to set it all off in the most optimal way possible.

> *"Ah be draymin' uv a shite Crissmuss, jus' like th' wans ah use' t' knaw."*

With many thanks to Mr Irving Berlin

Cubbert

Used to store and generally keep small(ish) things out of sight and out of mind on stoutly fitted internal shelving designed to support a multitude of items piled on them at random, a *cubbert* may be either a hollow, door-fronted recess set into a cottage wall or a piece of standing wooden furniture of modest dimensions.

> *'Ol' Mother Ubbert wooden ev ad much truck with th' cubbert in our front room up ome, cuz ours be vull of ever' kind uv rubbeesh ee kin 'magine. Us do push all th' traade in en layve ut there till ut do vall out agaane. There mus' be paapers on they shelfs what be ten year old er moo-er."*

Cuzzy-muzzy

A tiny ovoid form of seashell featuring a pleasing mottle of black spots set against a pinkish-brown background on its upper surface, and a glossy white underside pierced by a delicately ribbed slit. Some say that *cuzzy-muzzies* form a medium of currency used by tribesmen on certain Pacific islands, but unfortunately any similar consideration (although not for want of the boys trying) fails to find favour with Port Isaac shopkeepers.

> *"Th' bes' plaace t' come cross a cuzzy-muzzy round 'ere be in that pool jus' enshoo-er frum Tagg's Pit down be Port Gaaverne baych."*

With many thanks to Miss Elizabeth Bethell-Haydon of New Road

D

Daishels

Daishels are the characteristically long and aesthetically slender green leaves that surround the hollow succulence of a dandelion flower (or clock) stalk in a radial, fan-like arrangement. Such leaves are reputed to be edible and are occasionally gathered by Port Isaac boys for incorporation at home into a Sunday tea-time salad, failing takers for which the rabbit in its hutch out in the back garden will become the beneficiary. A gatherer of *daishels* must exercise all due care that he (or she) leaves the dandelions in place, since whether or not any of the flowers are picked deliberately or accidentally, it is well known that the picker will thereafter be subjected to involuntary nocturnal bed wetting consequences.

> *"Ol' Joe wuz up 'long th' ayges uv Wetha laane a while back pickin' daishels fer t' veed a's rabbuts. A got ol' ayps uv em, but trouble wuz th' maazed bugger picked th' bleddy dandy-lines s' well. A's guyne piss th' bed t'night fer shoo-er."*

Dam

Originally a condemnatory expletive owing much of its force to

67

the charming *cafflick* tradition of consigning sinners to hell, *dam* is these days more regularly employed as an expression of surprise by anyone who is suddenly confronted by the unexpected—although the ever-popular *bugger* linked to *bleddy* will reflect the intended sentiment just as well. Intellectuals (Port Isaac does not admit to many of those) classify *dam* as a "four-letter word"—erroneously as it turns out, since anyone versed in counting can easily calculate that the number of letters contained in *dam* is no more than three.

> *"When ah wuz guyne droo th' vicar's gardin t' taake a shoo-ert cut down th' 'ill, a come out braythin' vire en tol' me t' git 'way frum a's dam tetties. That wooden no way fer a vicar t' talk! Dam the ol' bugger t' th' devull a'zelf, thass what ah do zay!"*

Day

Day was not yesterday and nor will it be tomorrow—it is incontrovertibly today. Seven such *days* link up in sequence to form an amount of time known as a *wayke*. The names of the seven *days*, commencing with the Sabbath (so as not to lose sight of God commanding us all to remember it and keep it holy), are *Zundy, Mundy, Toosdy, Wensdy, Dursdy, Vrahdy, Zatdy*. Reference must also be made to certain popular *days* occurring more through random annual chance than as a result of formal routine—the former are known as *birfdys* and *ollydys*. *Birfdys* are welcomed whenever they occur whereas *ollydys* are most meaningful when they happen during the summer months.

> *"When be ee guyne come en vix me broke winda?"*
> *"Ah be guyne do un laater on day."*
> *"Thass what ee tol' me las' wayke!"*
> *"Aiz, en ah wooden be s'prised ef ah tells ee th' saame nex' wayke too, you!"*

Sacred to the memory of most Port Isaac tradesmen

68

Dee-er

A challenge issued by one person to another as emphatically as if it was a figurative mediaeval gauntlet thrown to the ground at the latter's feet by the former. A *dee-er* is always received and taken on in a spirit of reckless abandon flavoured with overtones of trepidation.

> *"Ah do dee-er ee t' climb up that tree s' far ez th' town craw's nest be th' top!"*
>
> *"Well, tez a bleddy long way up, but ah dee-er zay ah kin maake ut."*

Deerly

Deerly is a expression you use to imply a willingness to do something that has sadly (but not too sadly) been tainted by the fell clutch of your reluctance.

> *"Faather'd deerly like t' ev gone down t' Patsta on th' chapel outin, but a 'ad t' bank up a's tetties when th' time fer th' outin come 'round. Twuz like a zayed, us wooden've 'ad nart but grayne tetties in th' gardin when ut come round t' pull 'em ef they dedden git bank'd proper."*

Deeruvver

A mildly patronising expression of approval of the character of a young (the younger the better) girl—although ever more mature and for that matter quite elderly females are not necessarily exempt from consideration. The male equivalent of *deeruvver* is *deeruvvun*. The direct form of address is *deeruvvee*. The plural *deeruvvem* is also catered for. However, the first person singular *deeruvvme* and first person plural *deeruvvwe* are both frowned upon since they all too obviously imply a lack of modesty. It is of course well known that the people of Port Isaac are not only modest by nature but also have much to be modest about.

> "That little maid gived a ressytaashun uv "Come Inta th' Gardin Maud" down at th' ol' talint contest be th' Temp'rince All las' aybenin. Twuz rote be Lord zumbugger er other zo er did zay. Ah looked at th' maid en ah thought deeruvver, if thass th' bes' ee kin do ah dun't want yer Maud t' come into mah gardin, not now ner never."

With thanks to Miss Nora Keat of lower Front Hill

Deb'm

Cornwall's only neighbouring county, *Deb'm* is known in song as *"Deb'm Gloorius Deb'm"*. Such glory as *Deb'm* has, however, is a pale reflection of the majesty of the glory that is Cornwall. Since the common border separating the two counties is almost entirely coincident with the course of the River Tamar, the finest prospect that *Deb'm* provides for a traveller is a view over that river, looking towards the setting sun.

> "Ev ee ever taasted Deb'm crame buhy? Ah be guyne tell 'ee, us 'ad zum over be Tavvystock wance, en ef ee ever gits th' chaance to try uv ut, dun't ee do ut. Tez worsen addick's water, en ah could piddle stronger'n th' tay they gived we t' drink with our splitters."

Deffernt

When, even with the best will in the world (a rare commodity in Port Isaac) something (or someone) or other is reckoned to possess at least one individually unique characteristic (no matter how minor it may be) that he or she does not share with anything (or anyone) else, that characteristic is said to be *deffernt* to all of the others.

> "Ah s'pose that what with all th' im's en th' prayin, any wan

70

vicar oo taakes t' th' church uv a Zundy do ev t' be purty much th' zaame ez any other uv they bahbull-thumpin buggers, though when ut do come t' praychin, then vicars be s' deffernt frum aych other ez a crab do be frum a lopster."

Dellybole

The name of a dismal town set in its bleak place on an elevated blasted heath within distant sight of Port Isaac Bay. *Dellybole's* commanding location ensures exposure to every excess of wind and weather that the Atlantic Ocean can throw its way. The town's glum greyness of aspect comes as a result of most of its cottages and houses being built and roofed from the products of a gigantic slate quarry situated on its eastern outskirts. The quarry appears poised to swallow the town, and perhaps one day (with a bit of luck) it will. In the event that North Cornwall should ever require the administration of an enema, *Dellybole* is assuredly the place where the tube will be inserted.

> *"They do zay that a wayke in Dellybole be a ayp better'n a fortnight, but no time 'tall in that bleddy plaace do be better still. Ee do ev t' waitch out fer they oo lives up there—they talks deffernt t' we in Port."*

In fond memory of Mrs Emmeline (Em) Kent of Hartland Road

Diggin

You are in the act of *diggin* when you pay obsessive attention to your person through the medium of your fingers (acting individually or in unison) for (a) de-scaling crusting scabs on the skin; and (b) removing natural secretions which clog the nostrils, earholes, corners of the eyes, interstices between and within teeth, and every now and then the crack of the backside. Following success in *diggin* out some solid material, conventional practice demands that whatever is excavated should be both inspected and sniffed at prior to being consumed by way of mouth.

> *"That buhy be alwys diggin' in a's ears. Whassa like? There be more'n nuff filth in a's ear'oles to graw a raw uv tetties."*

Dinner time

The famous home meal named *dinner* is invariably sat down to every day between the noon hour and one o'clock in the afternoon. *Dinner time* is so engrained into the Port Isaac psyche that it has assumed the aura of a sacrosanct institution. For reasons which seem so implausible that they are all but impossible to comprehend, the *Likes uv They* not only sit down during *dinner time* to partake of what they describe as "lunch", but subsequently go on to eat what they call "dinner" in the late evening of the day. All of this serves to impress upon any Port Isaac boy the fact that there is no accounting for the taste of buggers like that.

> *"Us do ev roas' mayte be dinner time uv a Zundy, then us do ayt th' lef' overs cold fer dinner uv a Mundy. Other days fer dinner time us kin ev paasties, er pay zoop with figgy duff, er p'raps vried-up liver, er biled tripe. Ef there edden no mayte fer dinner coorse us ayts a dish uv tetties with oxo pour'd over em. Tedden a baad ol' life buhy!"*

Dip

The eternally popular tradition which involves partial immersion—rapidly followed by withdrawal—of a biscuit (or better yet the end of a slice of either bread and jam or bread and treacle) into a dish of tea. A good *dip* softens the texture and improves the taste of the item *dipped*. Inexperienced *dippers* often fail to appreciate that the critical success factors for a proper *dip* are timing and judgement if any collapse of the *dipped* item into the brew, there to sink to the bottom of the dish and suffer contamination from tea leaves when you try to suck it up afterwards, is to be avoided.

> *"Ef ah cooden dip me braid in tay, ah wooden give ee s'much ez th' time uv day fer a bit uv braid en jam."*

Dirty

The number that you get when you deduct ten from forty or alternatively multiply fifteen by two. *Dirty* additionally adds up to the total number of fingers and thumbs on the hands of three Port Isaac boys (barring accidental loss of any of the said digits), not to mention the condition of the same.

> *"'Ow old be ee buhy?"*
> *"Ah be dirty."*
> *"Aiz, ah can zee that be lookin' at yer faace en anns, but 'ow old be ee?"*

Dish

An open-topped receptacle typically made of china and other types of ceramic or pressed enamelled metal, a *dish* can be purchased in a range of sizes, shapes and decorative patterns certain to suit all tastes. Into a *dish*, with due consideration given to the appropriateness of its depth and diameter, tea may be poured for drinking; bread with warm milk and sugar can be combined to be eaten for breakfast; and a rice pudding will inevitably be concocted for serving as afters at *dinner time*.

> *"'Ere, will ee ev a dish uv tay?"*
> *"Thass proper, whabbee guyne giv us t' dip in un?"*
> *"Ebben got nart o' that fer ee!"*
> *"Ee kin kip yer bleddy tay then!"*

Divvy

Your *divvy* is at best a minuscule and at worst a derisorily intended financial return paid once annually by the Co-operative Wholesale Society (or CWS) to you in your capacity as a registered customer of that national chain's retail outlets. The value of *divvy* is nominally proportional to the sum you have spent at the Co-op during the preceding year. In Port Isaac the CWS shop is known as the *bleddy Kwop*—customers place great faith in holding on to an illusion that *divvy* signifies they are getting something for nothing.

> "Ah needs a bit uv chayze en a pat uv butter frum th' bleddy Kwop. When ee goes up to git uv em fer me, dun't ee fergit t' maake shoo-er that they writes th' proper mount down agin me divvy number, leb'm dree seb'm."

With thanks to Mrs Eleanor (Gran) Creighton of Canadian Terrace

Do

As a grammatical artifice of vital importance in promoting the smooth flow of verbal exchange, *do*, occasionally abbreviated to *d'*, is inserted into speech wherever support for a verb and the action which the verb calls for needs emphasis.

> "Ah do go mos' days downalong th' cliffs when th' gulls be layin', en ef ah d'be lucky ah do git to put zeverl aigs en me pockets afower ah d'come 'ome. They aigs be lovely t'ayt when they do be 'ard biled en mother d'chop uv em up t'ayve on noo braid."

Doo-er

A rectangular object chiefly fashioned from wood and having a pair of hinges attached to one of its long edges and a locking device incised into the other. *Doo-ers* are precisely set into orifices built-in for their reception in both the exterior and interior walls of cottages.

Once a *doo-er* is in place, its function is to control ingress and egress to the cottage and such rooms as the cottage may contain.

> *"Quick buhy, ah jus' zeed th' rent man comin up th' strayte. Us got t' git inzide, lock th' doo-er en 'ide under th' taable. Us ben't guyne anser th' bugger when a do knock on th' doo-er, en us wun't come out frum idin way till a be long gone."*

And, from the school playground—

> *"Ere buhy, ah got wan fer ee, when be a doo-er not a doo-er?"*
>
> *"Ah knaws ut, when ut do be a jar!"*
>
> *"Why dun't ee piss in un then, en drink me 'ealth?!"*

Dreckly

A word that could easily be used to extend the logical sequence of that well known playground skipping rope chant— *"This 'ear, nex' 'ear, zumtime, nivver."* Dreckly epitomises the ultimate degree of extension to which it is possible to stretch the elastic of time. It is founded on a well-meant intention to undertake an action—although not just now, maybe later, perhaps next week. Who knows and what is more who the *bleddy ell* cares? If recourse to invoking the concept of *dreckly* was to be abolished, many of Port Isaac's tradesmen, shopkeepers, fish jouders, builders and decorators would find themselves exposed in the eyes of their customers as being well and truly up shit creek without a paddle to fall back on.

> *"The vicar be lookin fer ee down be choir practice!"*
>
> *"Well ah did tell un a couple hour ago ah'd be comin' down dreckly."*
>
> *"Ah knaws that, but they oly rollin buggers ebben got no zense uv proper timin."*

Drepnybit

A coin of the realm which saw its best days years ago when it was being minted small and round out of noble silver. On rare occasions an example of such a *zilver drepnybit* may turn up in change from shopping, although most Port Isaac people only tend to come upon the one on which they break one of their few remaining teeth in its traditional token-of-good-luck place of concealment in a Christmas pudding. The here and now *drepnybit* is larger and thicker than the silver version, appearing to be minted from brass and provided with an awkwardly shaped dodecahedral rim. With its face value still equivalent to three copper pennies, the saving grace of the modern *drepnybit* is seen in the design on its tail which features a clump of the seapink flowers, known otherwise as thrift, which are so familiar along the cliff edges of Port Isaac Bay.

> "Ow much do ee want fer they flowers that ee've bin en pick'd up in th' bottoms buhy?"
>
> "Well missis, a small bunch uv primrosies'll cost ee a drepnybit, en a big wan do be zexpince, but fer th' vylits us wants a shillin'."

In fond memory of Mr Roger Keat of lower Front Hill

Drife

A meteorological circumstance linking clement sunshine to a light breeze, *drife* give assurance to the Port Isaac housewife that when her Monday morning washing is finally pegged out on the clothes line it will get dehydrated in short order. Unfortunately *drife* is seldom realised when it is most desired.

> "Th' wan thing ee kin be shoo-er uv when tez waishin' day ez that us shan't 'ev much drife t' 'elp kip 'way th' rain. Tez only possible t' wring jus' s' much water out uv th' cloze with th' mangle! Ah aates ut when ah ev t' pick in th' cloze when

they'm all drippin'. Still thass a burden us do ev t' bear, maid."

Droo

Anyone or anything proceeding unhindered from a given point of entry through to a corresponding exit is described as having gone all the way *droo*.

> *"Dun't ee coose downtown chawin' on that ol' bit uv stick! Ef ee wuz t' vall over t'would go right up droo th' roof uv yer mouf!"*

E

Ear

A period of time that begins at the stroke of midnight on the thirty-first day of December and continues unchecked until midnight strikes yet again when the subsequent thirty-first of December comes along. Optimism is normally high in Port Isaac as each *ear* starts, but the good feelings and personal resolutions that any such *noo ear* motivates usually survive only until the realities of life reassert themselves after no more than the passage of a few days at best. If you are familiar with the practice of counting you will know that the total number of days in one *ear* are three hundred and sixty-five, with the noted exception (since unfortunately there always has to be one rule or another to offend good order) that there are three hundred and sixty-six days to account for when the number of the *ear* is divisible by four.

> *"Th' zummer wuz a 'ole ayp better las' ear than a do be this ear. Dun't knaw why, but it do alwys zeem t' be that way. Things ben't never like what they wuz."*

A typical lament heard from Town Platt denizens

Ebben

The negative of *ev*. The *Likes uv They ev* got a lot, whereas the Port Isaac rank and file *ebben* got much at all. *Ebben* can also be written as *eb'm*.

> *"Will ee jus' taake a lookit a's cloze! Ah ebben never zeed th' likes uv ut. That poor bugger reely ebben got nart 'bout un t' maake ee think a do ev a couple coppers t' scraitch a's haass with."*

Edden

The present tense negative version of *be*, *edden* is synonymous with *ben't*. *Edden* may sometimes be inscribed as *ed'n* or perhaps even *idden*. Its past tense is *wooden*.

> *"Us wuz recknin' t' walk up Wetha Laane s'affnoon, but t'ev bin s' baad with th' wether that now we edden guyne, en ah kin tell ee, ah edden 'tall zorry. Oo in a's right mind wants t' go up t' Wetha anyroad rain er shine?"*

Ee

Nominally the second person singular pronoun, *ee* subject to context may equally be used for the second person plural pronoun. An example of the latter usage is *"you'm a 'ayp uv buggers all uv ee"*—although *"you ayp uv buggers you"* could be construed as getting rather more to the point.

> *"Ah tol' ee not t' do that! Whatever do 'ee think you'm doin'? Ee do git t' be a ole ayp wuss ever' day, en dam ee fer ut!"*

Emmets

A generic term to describe small, scurrying insects of the type of species that are devoted to keeping immediate company with large numbers of their own kind. Individuals in a gathering of *emmets* seem impelled to dart about in all directions simultaneously when their place of abode—as for example the stone under which they were residing—is suddenly disturbed. It is with reference to such group pattern behaviour that the descriptive noun *emmets* has come to be applied to the invading hordes of tourists and visitors from up the line that infest the Port Isaac scene during the summer months.

> *"All they red campions up be Bounds Cliff d' look reel purty, but tez terrubble t' walk droo em cuz they'm zwarmin with emmets that d' bite ee braave en ard on th' laigs ef ee ben't keerfull. Ah d' aate th' ol' ants th' wuss—emmets like they d' be all over ee in a mineet."*

Empt

The process of discharging as precipitately as possible the contents (whether solid or liquid being immaterial to the matter in hand as the whole lot has to go) of a domestic receptacle of any shape or size.

> *"Mother edden ere jus' now, er've gone down town t' empt out th' piss pot on th' baych."*

Endellion

The ultimate wooden-overcoated resting place for the majority of deceased Port Isaac residents. In spite of whether or not in life their affiliation was to Church or to Chapel or to none at all of the above, and notwithstanding that their characters were popularly reckoned to be good or bad or indifferent, *Endellion* is where they all end up. *Endellion* is a short name for St Endellion, a hamlet situated on the height of land two miles inland from the coast at Port Isaac. Within the clutch of this hamlet an extensive graveyard ready to receive the dearly departed surrounds the impossibly ancient Collegiate

Church of St Endelienta.

> *"Ah bin lookin' all 'round th' ol' 'arbour en Town Platt fer vishermen and ken't vind s'much ez wan. Kin ee tell me where they all do be?"*
>
> *"Caw missis, ee ben't guyne vind no proper vishermen down ere—they'm all up t' Endellion."*

In fond memory of Mr Harry (Arr) Oaten of Rose Hill

Er

The third person singular pronoun specifying a female. Under most circumstances, *er* is interchangeable with *she*.

> *"Ah zeed ol' Emmeline down be th' baaker's shop s'marnin. 'Er wuz lookin fer t' buy a caake uv Zunlight zope. Ole John be'ind th' counter did ask er what er wuz guyne use th' zope fer, cuz a cudden bleeve frum th' baissly look uv er that er wuz ever guyne off ome t' 'ev a waish."*

With thanks to Mr John Sherratt of Lundy Road

And as heard in the school playground—

> Headmaster: *"You there, who said you could do that?"*
> Boy (*pointing at class teacher in the distance*): *"Playze zur, she tol' me!"*
> Headmaster: *"She? She? Who do you think you are calling she?"*
> Boy: *"Playze zur, er over there!"*

In fond memory of "Boss" aka Mr C. Victor Richards

Ere

The opposite of *there*.

> *Ere ah come,*

Rusty Bum,
Doo, fower, zecks, aate—
Den ton!

The centrepiece chant of an impressively physical playground contact game

Errin

A modest sized species of fish celebrated as much for its oil-rich delicately-flavoured flesh as for its internal roe, which when of a durable oolitic texture forms a *dinner time* delicacy known as *pay raw*. When soft, *raws* are fodder only for the gulls. *Errins* unite in multitudinous shoals, a fortuitous habit that permits them to be netted by Port Isaac Bay fishermen in numbers exceeding many scores of thousands. As the *errins* are shaken from the nets on the harbour beach they shed glittering scales as prolifically as confetti at a decade's worth of weddings up at St Peter's church. A fresh *errin* is best eaten fried with a hunk of new bread close to hand. However, it is more commonly consumed following its transformation to a *kepper* in a smoke house. Alternatively, *errins* can be directly taken for eating from those typically flat, oval-shaped tins into which they are sealed in the company of tomato sauce to make a product referred to as *errinzin*.

> "*They errins ev got a foo t'many bones fer mah likin! T' git wan down me froat ah do ev t' chaw un up weth a gurt hunk uv braid en a dish uv tay. What ah do deerly love though do be the raws, speshly pay raws when they'm fried up be mother.*"

Esterdy

Esterdy is what today will be described as when tomorrow has arrived.

> "*Ah specks ah shall zee ee be th' maytin down Church*

82

Rooms laater on day."

"Git on with ee buhy, th' ol' maytin edden day, twuz esterdy!"

"Caw thass better! Ah ken't tell ee ow glad ah be t' ev missed the bugger! Tez so cold ez a church warden's charity down in they Rooms uv a aybenin."

Ev

The positive form of **ebben**. To *ev* something is to own or possess it—whether it benefits you or not, it is still yours. Some Port Isaac natives use *lef* in place of *ev*, purely as a matter of preference.

"Ah do ev t' go t' th' Zundy skool party t' git me tendince prize frum th' vicar. Zundy skool prizes be things like bahbulls en testimints en bleddy prayin' books. Oo th' ell wants they? Ee do ev t' be braave fer th' ol' church t' raid droo they buggers, but ayben though ah should like somthin' deffernt ah do still lef to taake what ah gits gived."

F

Fayled

The downhill state of your health according to an instant eyeball diagnosis by an acquaintance you meet up with who hasn't seen you for a while. He or she will not only take great pains to inform you that you have *fayled* but will also manage to make you believe that your prospects for staying clear of *Endellion* for much longer are not good.

> "*Ere, tez ee, edden ut? 'Ow be ee buhy? Ah ebben zeed ee fer leas' a coupla 'ears! Tez proper t' zee ee 'gain!*"
> "*Caw buhy, ee've fayled, ebben ee!*"

With thanks to Mr Clifford "Digger" Sloggett of Hartland Road

Farty

Farty is what you get when you add thirty to one third of thirty. Lovers of popular music will recall that *farty* is the age at which Miss Sophie Tucker in her role as "the last of the red hot mommas" informed an ever-admiring public that life begins.

> "*Talk 'bout mutton dressed up like lamb! Er wun't zee farty 'gain this zide uv Endellion, en ah dee-er zay er've bin pullin'on*

84

farty fer long nuff now that ef er' wuz a oss erd've ad time t'
plough all uv a seb'm aacre vield den times over."

Festyvill

Any extraordinarily special event which is only celebrated, much
to the disappointment of the boys of Port Isaac, on a once-annual
basis. Although the boys find every *festyvill* worth waiting for, time
always seems to hangs heavy on their hands as the great day draws
tantalisingly nigh. A *festyvill* takes place following substantial
advance planning and is likely to involve its celebrants, inter alia,
donning either their best clothes or fancy dress; indulging in
community sing-songs; and consuming much strong tea, sandwiches
with the crusts left on, currant buns, wobbly jellies and (with luck)
a few slices of cake.

> *"Nex' Zundy down be th' Town Platt they be guyne t' ev th'*
> *Skarrick chapel arviss festyvill uv th' zay. Tez alwys a braave*
> *ol' thing—chapel do ev they proper 'ims fer zingin with the*
> *wind blawin' over ee. Mos' uv th' vishermen turns out, en tez*
> *zum zight t' zee they buggers prayin' cuz there edden wan*
> *'mong 'em that ever do zet a's vit on th' floo-er of church nor*
> *chapel alike any other time cep fer foonerulls."*

Ferrickin

A process of persistent investigation which, if the truth were to
be told, is normally associated with no genuine expectation of the
investigator achieving a successful outcome.

> *"Whenever ah bin in er 'ouse twuz t' vind er ferrickin 'bout*
> *in cubberts en in be'ind chairs, s'well's under th' taable. Er*
> *wooden never tell ah what all er ferrickin wuz fer, though ah*
> *specks that t' ferrick like 'er do t'will ev t' be rats that er do be*

tryin t' vind, cuz I do knaw there edden bugger all else in any uv 'er cubberts."

In fond memory of Miss Maud Lark of Tintagel Terrace

Figgy Duff

A traditional loaf-shaped culinary masterpiece prepared by integrating measured quantities of suet, water, self-raising flour and either currants or raisins (or better yet both of these highly desirable dried fruits). Brought to peak condition when boiled in the secure embrace of a tightly closed muslin bag, a *figgy duff* forms an ideal complement to a knuckle of ham in *pay zoop*. Port Isaac gourmets consider it to be such bad form when a *figgy duff* goes light on dried fruit content that they are certain to make their displeasure known to the cook.

"Th' zight uv this ere knife, who be maade uv th' vinest Sheffield stayle, be garinteed t' maake a figgy duff tremble in a's bag, en a laig o' mutton jump off th' taable en 'ide away in the cubbert!"

With many thanks to the one and only Mr Tom Brown of "Lenhareen" in upper Fore Street.

Flem

A gelatinous form of human expectorant with an unctuously cloying texture, *flem* reaches the light of day in shades of colour favouring variants of green, brown and yellow. *Flem* is sourced in the lungs. With an explosively guttural liquid rattle a prime exponent of the art is able to elevate *flem* up through his throat and, with an expert flick of the tongue, eject it out through his mouth in the manner of a high-speed missile. This process overall is sometimes referred to as *uckin* or *gobbin*, the difference being that *uckin* as a rule is less noisy and often more surreptitiously executed than *gobbin*.

"T' start off th' day ah do alwys ev a good ol' coff fer zeverl mineets when ah waakes up in th' marnin. Then, wance ah gits t' uck op a braave ayp uv flem inta th' jerry ah do be reddy fer me fust fag!"

With many thanks to Mr Frank Eade of Middle Street

Flemmenturd

A bottled curd-like preserve which, irrespective of being either home-made or **boughten**, owes its unpleasant flavour and biliously yellow hue to the inclusion of lemons in its recipe. *Flemmenturd* spread on a slice of bread is considered by many Port Isaac boys to constitute an unwelcome assault on the versatility of even their taste buds. Their imperative of evading all *flemmenturd* on offer at either breakfast, **dinner time** or tea time smacks of an impressive stoicism in the face of inevitable parental censure.

"Zaffern caake en yaiss caake do be me faavrites fer tay, en ah do deerly like spunje caake s'well, 'cept when flemmenturd gits put in th' middle. Ah kin tell ee ah wooden never ayt nart with flemmenturd in ut. Tez wuss'n zeed caake! I do zooner ayt shite."

Flibberty Jibbert

A descriptive term applied to a girl whose allegedly erratic behaviour and looseness of personal deportment are not regarded by her contemporaries as being anything out of the ordinary, but are reckoned to lie somewhere outside the pale of acceptability in the opinion of most of her elders and betters.

"That maid do ev idees outzide uv er staation, en purty many do wonder whass guyne become uv er in a foo ears time. Er do ask s' many maazed kweschins uv ee! Then er goes off gaadin 'bout all over th' plaace s'ef er did awn all uv ut. Er do be a

flibberty jibbert en no mistaake! Ah tol' er off las' wayke en er gived me zuch a mouthful uv chayke ah would uv laaced er laigs fer er ef er adden coosed off."

Floo-er

An important architectural feature of the majority of cottages, houses and commercial establishments, a *floo-er* is normally (although in Port Isaac cottages not quite always) planar and level in nature. Its function is to provide support for the respective legs of furniture, people, and dogs and cats among others. The usual materials from which a typical *floo-er* is likely to be made are either wood or cement-based aggregates. The surface of a *floo-er* is frequently covered in *canvas*, although for those who can afford it some form of carpet will also do the job. An alternative name for *floo-er* is *planchen*, but as the latter is considered archaic even in a place like Port Isaac, the more modern former is much to be preferred.

> *"Ee kin ayt yer dinner off mother's floo-er, but ah kin tell ee that ef ee wuz t' g'win nex' doo-er, ee wooden ayben want t'ayt off th' taable. Th' nex' doo-er floo-er be covered with fag ends, daid matches en vish scaales, en ez fer th' vire plaace in there, well ah dun't want t' tell ee ow much dried flem en gob be stuck all 'round ut."*

Flora

A free-for-all procession masquerading as a communal folk dance which takes place in the streets of Port Isaac on at least a once-weekly basis during the summer. Musical accompaniment of a curious tone is provided at the head of the procession by a group of amateur musicians who together make up the St Breward silver band. Any shortcomings in the performance of cornet, clarinet, big trombone, fiddle, cello, bassoon, flute and euphonium are more than effectively disguised by the constant beat of a big bass drum. Needless to say, participation in the *Flora* spectacle is as popular with *emmets* as it is with the native born.

> *Charlie zayed t'me wan day*
> *"Kin ee daance th' Flora?"*
> *Charlie zayed t'me wan day*
> *"Kin ee daance th' Flora?"*
> *"Aiz ah kin, with a naice young man,*
> *Aiz ah kin, with a naice young man,*
> *Aiz ah kin, with a naice young man,*
> *Ah kin daance th' Flora!"*

With many thanks to the unknown lyricist of the "Cornish Flora Dance"

Forthy

A description of the character of a child who has concluded that being seen and not heard is not at all what he or she wants to do, and who has therefore elected to offer his or her unsolicited opinions to his or her elders and betters and to let the cards of retribution fall where they may.

> *"That cheel tol' me that ah wuz too much fer mindin' th' bizniss uv others, en t'wood be better fit ef ah wuz to go 'ome en look t'me awn affairs fer a chaange. Er be too bleddy forthy fer er awn good! Th' skool taychers do zay er's guyne go far, en where ah do be consarned th' futhur tez, th' better!"*

Fox

The surname of a Guy who is jutifiably worshipped by Port Isaac boys when they remember, remember the fifth of November. Each year on the evening of that historic day a crudely made effigy of *Mr Guy Fox* is paraded through the streets by a gang of his young admirers in a vain quest to solicit donations of a penny on his behalf

89

from the miserable buggers they always seem to meet up with. To add insult to injury to *Mr Guy Fox*, when darkness falls the boys place his effigy at the summit of a very large pile of combustible material and proceed to turn the whole thing into his funeral pyre.

> *"I do reely wish Guy Fox wuz ere now. A would uv bin a champeen fer the Likes uv We! Us could uv ad un go in Waybridge t' shove a foo bar'ls o' gunpowder under they bleddy buggers in th' council!"*

In fond memory of Mr Jim (Bweddy Buggos) Honey of Temple Bar

Frayd

A highly tactful yet rather insincere admission of your reluctance to undertake an action which (to your secret delight) is likely to be to the detriment of one or more of your most despised acquaintances or neighbours.

> *"Th' money do be a bit shoo-ert 'day, do ee think ee could let me ev a cupple poun tetties on tick?"*
>
> *"Frayd not missis, frayd ah ken't do nart fer ee. Ee do still awe me vahvepence dree farthins from doo munce back fer they graynes I let ee ev then, en ah ben't maade uv munny."*

Fust

In prime position. To be *fust* is to be the best of the bunch, ahead of everything and of every other participant in an activity, event, planned action campaign, arrangement or selection.

> *Tez th' fust week in May,*
> *When th' gulls begins t' lay.*

In fond memory of Mr Terry (Tibby) Thomas of Church Hill

90

Fuzz

A shrub that flourishes in impenetrable and riotous thickets along the gentler slopes of the Port Isaac and Port Gaverne valleys. The chief attributes of a *fuzz* bush are its severe prickliness, the veritable sun-burst of bright yellow flowers that open during the spring of the year and a dramatically incendiary rate of high-speed conflagration when the bush is set alight either accidentally or deliberately.

> *"That ol' laady who do zit in th' fust poo in church ever' Zundy, us do alwys ev t' waitch out fer er. Er dun't like we buhys. We do call er Fanny Fuzz Bush, cuz er's like a fuzz bush in Aperl, all shaw on th'outzide, sharp's a tack belaw, en s' like ez not t' taake yer aid off ef ee should vire er up."*

With many thanks for the memory of the genteel Miss Furze of lower Trewetha Lane

Fynen

A word that anyone in Port Isaac with an aversion to applying the adjective **bleddy** as a means of adding emphasis to a noun (surprisingly enough, a few **bleddy-o-phobes** do exist) can use as a substitute in good heart.

> *"Ah jus' come 'ome frum Waybridge, en ben't ah playsed! Ah never zeed rain pissin' down like twuz in there! Ah tell ee maid, twuz fynen emptin down!"*

G

Gaadin

When you go out *gaadin,* or as some say, go off *on th' gaad,* you undertake an excursion to pursue social activities designed to satisfy purely sybaritic motives. The frequency of your *gaadin* promotes the intensity of disapprovingly critical assessment that you receive from those miserable old buggers whose predilection for having fun is, unlike yours, strictly limited.

> *"Ah do veel s' zorry fer a's poo-er mother, zittin 'ome in the aybenin while a do go out on th' gaad. T' maake ut s' much wuss a's off gaadin bout with maidens er did zay. A's guyne braake er 'art. Er dedden raise un fer that!"*

With many thanks to Mrs Ethel Brown of Trewetha Lane

Gaake

A form of direct scrutiny that you carry out out in association with wide-eyed assiduity. It is also common for a *gaake* to generate an expression of open-mouthed incredulity in which your lolling tongue holds centre stage. People who *gaake* tend to see much while comprehending little.

"Th' bes' plaace t' zit in our classroom be th' desk in th' back carner be th' winda. That do 'low we t' gaake et th' gulls outzide en fergit bout th' taychur guyne on en on bout bugger all up front be th' blackboo-erd."

In appreciation of Mr Willie Chadband of Trelights

Gannit

A gourmand. A ***proper gannit*** is proficient in swallowing or bolting down any or all of the comestibles on his dinner plate without recourse to chewing, by which means he eliminates any delay in presenting his empty plate for a second helping (should it be available and should the menu have been to his liking). *Gannit* technique is particularly useful when tripe is on the menu—but no second helpings of shite like that please!

"Me granfer do be zome gannit you! A kin fineesh up all uv a's mayte en tetties afower th' echo uv a's zucking up th' graavy ev died 'way!"

With many thanks to the peerless comedian Mr Ted Ray

Gar

An expletive as benign as it is widely used, *gar* provides the pious of Port Isaac with an acceptable means of circumventing the mandate of the Third Commandment. *Lawksamussy* however! Whether or not the *Lard* will hold the perpetrators of *gar* guiltless remains open to debate even unto this day.

Matthew, Mark, Luke en John,
Maade a paasty ten vit long.
They crimped un wance, they pricked un dwice,
Aw mah Gar, 'twuz vull uv mice!

93

Matthew, John, Mark en Luke,
Put the paasty in t' cook.
Th' vire went out, th' mayte stayed raw,
They 'ayved th' paasty out th' doo-er.

Matthew, Luke, John en Mark,
Picked up th' paasty when twuz dark.
John was zad, and Mark verloorn—a
Bit come off th' right zide carner.

John, Mark, Luke en Matthew,
Only cooked th' pasty aff droo.
They laid th' paasty on th' taable,
En ayt zuch bits ez they wuz aable.

An augmentation of a traditional playground rhyme

Gardin

A lovesome thing, God wot! A *gardin* is a patch of land, normally covering only a modest area and typically located within easy walking distance of its owner's cottage hearth. In a *gardin's* well-tended soil a tried and tested variety of vegetables is cultivated for domestic consumption. The *gardin* soil is treated by he who tills it with infinitely more care than his neighbours ever see him portioning out to his wife and family. A *gardin* situated more distantly from the home is referred to as a **lotmint** even though the latter's function is identical to the former's.

"Will ee come inta th' gardin Maud?
Fer th'ol' black bat night bugger ev flawn.
Wun't ee come inta th' gardin Maud?
Ah do be 'ere be th' bleddy gaate on me awn!"

With apologies to Alfred, Lord Tennyson

Gardyin

Published in Bodmin and distributed throughout the North Cornwall district for sale every Thursday morning, the *Gardyin* is quite simply the district's finest weekly newspaper—no matter that it is the only such publication of its kind put together on native soil. Nay, let us be be even more categoric about the quality of the *Gardyin* by favourably comparing its newsworthiness with that of any of its counterparts in any other region of dear old Cornwall. Entirely to its editor's satisfaction, the *Gardyin* chronicles the life and times of the rural communities that it serves. It rarely has an opportunity to carry out in-depth reporting on juicy local scandals, but when it does, well, Thursdays in places like Port Isaac become positively enhanced when the *Gardyin* is delivered.

> *"Ef you'm passin uv th' paaper shop kin ee git me a Gardyin playze? Twuz ol' Jack's fooneral las' week, en ah wants t' raid bout oo wuz at un. Jack wuz a miser'ble bugger all a's life, en fer they what went up t'Endellion t' zee un off ah be sartin they wuz jus wantin t' maake shoo-er a wuz proper en daid."*

In fond memory of Mrs Rowe, newsagent of lower Fore Street

Gash

When you judge that someone possesses more than his or her proper share of something of substance, the perceived excess is known as *gash*. All *gash* is fair game to be extracted from its owner through dint of begging, borrowing or, when push comes to shove, a more dastardly method.

> *"Ee do ev a luv'ly gardin there buhy, en thass a reel fine raw uv runner baynes that you'm pickin'. Ah wooden mind zum ef 'ee ad a foo gash wans, cuz ah kin zee there do be moo-er angin' there reddy t' pick than ee wants fer yer dinner."*

Gee-gees

Gee-gees are equine animals carrying diminutive creatures referred to as *jockuys* on their backs. One *gee-gee* can be distinguished from another by observing the unique colour and pattern of the garments worn by its *jockuy* when compared to the others. Trained *gee-gees* compete in races over fixed distances at celebrated *up th' line* venues for the purpose of attracting unsuccessful wagers on the likelihood of their coming first, second or third past the finishing post. With respect to those who wager, few are chosen but many are galled.

> *"Oo be that ammerin on me doo-er?"*
> *"Tez me buhy, ere t' c'leck yer rent!"*
> *"Afower ah opens th' doo-er, kin ee tell us what gee-gee won the dree-dirty up be Noomarkit?"*
> *"Ah ebben got no idee—tedden what ah be ere fer!"*
> *"Ee should be in th' knaw buhy, yer rent money do be runnin on un!"*

With thanks to the late great Jimmy "Aye-aye, that's yer lot!" Wheeler

Gintry

A privileged class of people whose hereditary claim to rank is, as Mr Robert Burns put it so incisively, "but the guinea stamp". The *gintry* make no secret of the fact that they regard the Port Isaac *Likes uv We* not only as the great unwashed but as having furthermore been placed on this earth to serve them and to be otherwise disregarded to the ultimate limit of possibility. Should a member of the *gintry* be faced with no option except to socialise with one or more of the *Likes uv We*, an instinctive defensive mechanism common to them all displays a form of patrimony that could be seen as rather amusing if it wasn't so *bleddy* insulting.

> *"Me mother wuz in sarvice t' Adm'rull Rogers down be Rock,*

waitin' on th' bugger anns en vit fer 'ears. Frum what er tol'
me, gintry like a do be mayner'n a church warden oo gives the
poo-er only what a gits frum wipin th' church with th' 'airs uv
a's haass. Mother vound a ol' ayp uv wine bottles in a zeller
covered op with cobwaybs en caw, th' bleddy Adm'rull was
some maazed bout ut when er dustid 'em off."

In appreciation of Miss Betty Creighton of Canadian Terrace

Giveesh

A quality accorded to you by your peers as a result of your having
demonstrated that it is more blessed to give than to receive, even
when you don't really believe this homily for a single moment. What
you know for certain is that in Port Isaac an ostensibly *giveesh*
person will always be sowing seeds aimed at reaping the fruits of an
eventual quid pro quo.

> *"Ee dedden never let 'er 'ev aff yer swyate rashin—you'm*
> *zome giveesh you!"*
> *"Well, 'twuz lickrish allsoo-erts this wayke en ah dun't like*
> *they s' much so any bugger be welcome to em! Coorse ah knaws*
> *er's guyne git toffees on th' rashin zome time en ah deerly loves*
> *they. Ah be guyne look fer me share frum 'er then, en ah shall*
> *taake any gash chocklit that 'er'll ev on th' zide too!"*

Glaass

A scientific instrument used for measuring changes in atmospheric
pressure. A *glaass* features a graduated column of quicksilver sealed
within a narrow glass tube. Port Isaac fishermen are well-versed in
reading the famous *glaass* set into the front wall of Pawlyn's fish
cellars down at the Town Platt. These piscatorial worthies are able
to inspect the *glaass* and forecast inaccurate weather conditions at
the drop of a flat cap.

"Ah be thinkin' uv guyne out zay s'aybenin. What do th'
glaass zay?"

"Ee dun't need t' bother 'bout no glaass buhy! Jus' do ee look
out zay! Ef ee kin zee Lundy Island tez guyne rain, en ef ee
ken't zee th' bugger, then tez alreddy rainin'!"

"Thass all well en good, but ah knaws ee zeed the glaas
down be Pawlyn's early on s'marnin en ah wuz jus' wond'rin
what a zayed!"

"Well ah tell ee, you, a dedden zay nart. Dun't ee knaw th'
ol' glaass ken't spayke?"

Gleeb

A field securely surrounded by a hedge, located adjacent to a
churchyard and accessed from the said churchyard via a narrow
gate, the rusty hinges of which yield reluctantly and noisily to the
shoulder. *Gleeb* land is often kept fallow, in which capacity it may
be used either for grazing livestock or for growing a crop of coarse
seasonal hay. Its long-term destiny lies in undertaking the suitably
consecrated task of absorbing the overflow of dearly departed from
the adjoining churchyard once the latter has filled up.

"Ere, sextin, whatever do appen t' all th' daid flowers ee do
taake off th' graaves? Ow do ee manage t' kaype th' graaveyard
s' clayne?"

"Tez aisy nuff buhy, Ah jus' ayves 'em all over th' ayge into
th' gleeb vield!"

Godfaather en Godmother

These are honorary titles awarded by mandate of the Book of
Common Prayer to the reluctant volunteers who have been
impressed into taking on a job formality related to the baptism
of an infant. The function of a *Godfaather en/er Godmother* is to

promise and vow three things in the name of the said infant while presumably entertaining for a moment the intention to hold the infant accountable for his or her certain lapses from the promises and vows in later years. The infant has no say in the matter at all. The *Godfaather en Godmother* titles are enshrined in the expletive, *"mah Godfaathers en Godmothers!"*, which is normally invoked by a real mother when she condemns the behaviour of her offspring.

> *"Whabbee yer naame?"*
>
> *"N er M." (N er M—whabbee that fer Cryssaake?)*
>
> *"Oo gived ee yer naame?"*
>
> *"Mah Godfaathers en Godmothers be me baptism, wherein ah wuz maade a member uv Cryse, a cheel uv God, en a hineriter uv the kingdim uv eb'm."*

With apologies to the compilers of the Book of Common Prayer

Grafted

The cumulative knock-on effect of allowing your body to go unwashed for a period of time long enough to invest it with a state of superficially grimy grace that is totally repellent to water.

> *"Ol' Ruy dun't never wear no collars that ah ever zeed. A's neck do be s' grafted that a ken't kaype a collar clayne fer vahve mineets. Dun't knaw when a's las' baff night wuz, but t'wooden this zide uv Ayster!"*

In memory of Capt Roy May of Roscarrock Hill

Graaper

A small three-pronged implement made of iron. When fastened to one end of a suitable length of rope, the other end of which is attached to the bow ring of a small punt, a *graaper* dropped overboard in shallow water forms a quite effective anchor.

"Th' oo-er did braake in 'aff when ah wuz kaypin th' ol' punt en scullin uv un 'round th'arbour. Ah ayved out th' graaper but there wooden no paynter on th' bugger, s'that dedden 'elp 'tall."

Graynes

A multi-purpose word related to a wide range of vegetables chiefly recognised for (a) their leafiness, and (b) a universal tendency to be over-boiled on the domestic stove. The distinctive colour of *graynes* is what you get when blue is blended with yellow. *Graynes* of any kind—inclusive of *cabbitch, brockla, cut-en-cum agaane, collyflower, turnup aids, pays, runner baynes, broad baynes, brussulls* and *lettiss*—give rise to resigned expressions of repulsion when they appear on the *dinner time* plates of most of the younger residents of Port Isaac.

> *"Ayt op yer graynes buhy!"*
> *"Dun't like 'em!"*
> *"There do be cheldern starvin' in Afreeka oo'd be only too glad t'ayt they."*
> *"Well why dun't ee zend th' bleddy graynes t'Afreeka then?"*

Or, in a skipping rope rhyme chanted in the school playground:

> *Aiz zur, no zur,*
> *Thankee zur, playze zur,*
> *Up a duck's be'ind*
> *Ee'll vind grayne pays zur!*

Grizzle

A sentiment of personal well-being which sets a positive cast to both the mouth and eyes of those who have it. A *grizzle* is often associated with the receipt of gratifying news, and is known to appear instantly when the first note of the "ITMA" signature tune is heard on the wireless.

"Ah went up t' th' vestry en tol' th' vicar that a's fly buttons wuz undone."

"Whaddid a zay to ee?"

"A tol' me that ef ah dedden wipe th' grizzle off me faace a'd wipe un off fer me."

Gudfurry

An expression of justification intended to persuade, cajole and ultimately coerce a Port Isaac boy into conquering the unpalatable. No matter how bad something may appear to be to a boy at first sight it is certain to be no better when he tackles it on the understanding that *tez gudfurry*.

"Ah ken't ayt this ere biled tripe mother, et always do maake ah zick!"

"Ah dun't care bout that, jus' do ee git ut down ee, tez gudfurry!"

Gug

A natural rock cavity, the dimensions of which are typically high, narrow and extensive with respect to inner penetration, a *gug* is formed through the persistent marine erosion of a cliff face along a line of geological weakness. The ultimate consequence of the process may be either a cove-like re-entrant open to the sky above, or a darkly mysterious cave.

"Th' gug on t'other zide uv th' aystern braakewater do go a reel long way in, zo us needs candles t' zee where we'm guyne when us gits a fair way back in un. Then us do ev t' waitch th' time which edden aizy when us ebben got no clock, cuz the ol' tide do be comin' op, en a dun't wait fer no bugger."

Gull

The quintessentially familiar grey and white feathered bird of cliffs, seas and rooftops, whose enduring presence in great numbers in and around coastal villages like Port Isaac is subject to a long-held mystique similar to that attributed to the ravens of the Tower of London. The name *gull* is applied in Port Isaac to a species that guidebooks refer to as the herring gull. Its cousin, the greater black-backed gull, numerically fewer although still significant around the Bay, is popularly known as the *black annie*. *Gulls* are extremely gregarious birds and in recent years have become increasingly addicted to performing an invaluable role in scavenging and generally cleaning up waste strewn around the village streets and harbour beach by *emmets* who don't know any better.

> *"A gull do lay dree aigs fer 'aitchin'. Ef ee kin git t' th' ol' nest when there do be doo aigs in un en then taake 'way wan, er'll kaype on layin jus' like a fowl cuz er edden no good fer countin uv em. Thass th' bes' way fer ee t' ev a gull's aig reg'lar fer yer tay in the fust part uv May month."*

In fond memory of Mr Edgar "Old Egger" Bate of Church Hill

Gurt

A word employed to add emphasis to any observations you make on people, objects or events that are seen to be blessed with size, power, strength, substantial external dimensions and so on and so forth. *Gurt* enhances grandeur that is quite obviously grand in its own right in the first place.

> *"They dree Smith brothers, they'm gurt great buhys. Ole Stanley ev got a pair uv anns on un that looks gurt nuff t' pick up a hunderd uv tetties aizy in aych wan."*

In fond memory of Messrs Charlie, Clarence and Stanley Smith of "The Wrennery", Port Gaverne

Gut

A narrow strait or channel of open water, not necessarily navigable, a *gut* separates a coastal promontory from an offshore seastack or sentinel rock which, way back in the mists of geological erosion, was itself a part of the promontory.

> *"Mos' uv we larned t' zwim in th' Cassle Rock gut down be Port Gaverne when we wuz small. The big buhys use t' taake we t' th' gut en ayve us in th' zay en layve us there. 'Twuz zink er zwim, en purty near all uv us dedden want t' zink ef us could 'elp ut. Mind ee now, they only ayved we in when twuz calm zays so t'wooden s' baad reely. Ef ee wuz ayved in th' bleddy gut in a ruff zay ee'd uv 'ad ut fer sartin."*

Guyne

A useful word allowing you to advise anyone of your intention to depart from one place in order to proceed to another, or not to go at all as the case may be.

> *"Ullo buhy, where be guyne?"*
> *"Guyne Zundy skool. 'Ow bout yerzelf? Be ee comin?"*
> *"Git on with ee buhy, ah ben't guyne! Th' zay be out en ah do be off down baych t' git winkles off th' rocks fer faather's tay."*

H

H

The aspirate aich does come in andy sometimes!

Haass

A generally gleefully celebrated anatomical feature located at the rear of the body, a *haass* consists of a pair of large and quite fleshy (sometimes impressively large and outstandingly fleshy) appendages known as *chaykes* which meet in order to cover and protect a rounded orifice (the *haassawl*) from which a range of amusing internally generated wind-driven sounds may (with luck) be emitted and become especially entertaining to experience when they occur involuntarily. A *haass* is not often spoken of as such in polite company, euphemisms such as *be'ind* and *backzide* being preferred, even though the vicar himself has got one.

> *Ah 'ad a little donkey,*
> *Ah fed un on graass.*
> *En ef a wooden ayt ut;*
> *Ah shoved ut up a's haass.*

With many thanks to Mr Billy "Pom Pom" Brown Sr of upper Dolphin Street

And, not forgetting a riddle from the school playground:

> "Ere, oo wuz ut in th' Bahbull what ad a 'lastic backzide?"
> "Dun't knaw, oo wuz ut then?"
> "Twuz Jayzus, cuz a tied a's haass t' a tree en walked inta Juhroosalim!"

And finally:

> "Ah bin tol' that 'Enery 'All ev got doo brothers!"
> "Ev a reely! Whabbee they called then?"
> "Haassawl en bugger all!"

With many thanks to Mr Trevor Platt of Canadian Terrace

Helba

A flexible joint at the junction of your forearm with your upper arm, the *helba* promotes ready articulation of movement of the former. A *helba* is also referred to as a "funny-bone", although anyone who has ever received a sharp blow from a blunt instrument on one of his or her *helbas* will no doubt consider such a name to be singularly inappropriate.

> "Ah jus' dun't knaw what t' maake uv yer cloze. You'm out t' haass and out t' helba, en the bes' ah kin zay fer ee ez that yer coat maakes ee look like a zack o'shite tahd up ugly."

Heller

A title bestowed upon a boy—whether he is big or small making no difference—by his long-suffering elders and betters as a direct consequence of their jaundiced appreciation of his propensity to conduct a career of unrestrained havoc-wreaking mischief. All affected elders and betters entertain a fervent desire to grab hold of the collar of a designated *heller* when a stout stick is within their easy reach. Needless to say, a boy categorised as a *heller* is justifiably proud of his achievements. Such a title is hard earned and is to be cherished.

> *"That buhy d' be a reel heller, alwys rampaagin droo me gardin en up en down th' strayte outzide me 'ouse! Th' little bugger kin rin vaaster'm me, but ah shall bide me time t' coose after un en git t' tan a's haass wan day good en proper."*

Hunderd

A *hunderd* is theoretically the mathematical sum of ninety-nine plus one. However, in every-day working practice it has come to be enshrined as the avoirdupois weight measure of precisely one hundred and twelve pounds of a bulk commodity like coal that can be typically confined in a stout hessian sack in order to present it as being fit for sale.

> *"Ol' 'Arold th' cawl man do wet a's cawl down bezide a's garridge in Wetha Laane where a do kaype a's dee-livvery lorry. That do mayne that fer aych hunderd uv cawl we do buy frum un a fair bit uv the weight do be water! T'wooden be s' baad but fer th' fack that mos' uv th' res' uv th' hunderd do be slaate en slack."*

Hurted

The physical condition of someone who has sustained an injury of a rather trivial nature, but who nevertheless takes advantage of the golden opportunity he has been provided with to complain vociferously about how much he has been *hurted* to anyone he can inveigle into listening to his tale of woe.

> *"Tedden no good t' play with that buhy. A's always vallin'down en zayin' that a've bin hurted when nart ev appened to un 'tall! Then a's mother do come out coosin after we oo wuz playin with un. If ee do ask me, a's a proper Mary en no mistaake bout ut!"*

In fond memory of Mrs Elsie Richards of the Schoolhouse

I

Ile

An inflammable liquid gifted with properties of volatility, pungent odour and an uncanny ability to instantly invest itself into and over everything in the vicinity of a spillage, no matter how restricted the spillage may be. Domestic *ile,* popularly known as **parrafeen** in Port Isaac, is obtained from a bulk storage tank kept out at the back of the **bleddy Kwop** or Chapman's grocery shop. *Ile* is used to feed the wicks of smoky lamps and evil-smelling portable stoves that respectively shed dim light and establish local pockets of warmth in the cottage environment.

> *"Zumtimes ef th' vire wun't draw proper when ah lights un, ah ayves on a thimble er too uv ile t' 'elp un out. Ee do ev t' be careful ow tez done mind, zo ez not t' ev the cawl blaw out in yer faace, er ev the vlaames go up en zet a chimbly vire guyne!"*

Im

A *im* is a religiously themed lyric set to music, as often as not with a much-holier-than-thou feel fully incorporated. *Ims* are written to

107

be sung by Church and Chapel congregations battling to achieve the precise co-ordination of words and music that were envisaged by the writer/composer. With a bit of luck, and when available, the musical accompaniment of piano, harmonium or organ can help to carry most *ims* through to the grateful "Amen" with which each and every one concludes.

> "*Th' las' im us zung wuz "Onward Crischin Soljers, marchin as t' war". I ben't s' shoo-er bout th' marchin part though. Us did all start off zingin roun 'bout th' zaame time, but afore th' fust verse wuz vineeshed th' congreegaashin wuz all over th' plaace, en be th' end uv un ayben th' orgin wuz zeverl paaces in front uv th' Amen! Twuz all s' out uv step us could uv cross'd a wood bridge without shiverin a zingle timber uv th' bugger.*"

Iyern

A metallic implement vital to the well-being of the cottage home. An *iyern* consists of a basal plate of smooth, rust-free metal surmounted by a facilitating handle for its proper manipulation. Once the base plate has been heated up to an appropriate temperature by means of prolonged contact with a source of transferable heat (such as the hotplate of the stove or the front of the fireplace grate), an *iyern* is taken in hand and used to commit a to-and-fro motion on top of an item of recently washed (and dried) clothing or bedding in an attempt to drive wrinkles and creases out of the fabric. The name *iyern* is derived from a ferrous element with the chemical symbol Fe which features so prominently in its manufacture. Oddly enough, the names of no other tools and trappings for domestic use bear any reference whatsoever to the material(s) from which they are made, assuming of course that a wooden spoon has been discounted.

> "*Us 'ad a gurt zet uv iyern raylins longzide th' skool, but*

th' bleddy council come en cahrr'd em off fer war scrap. Ah dedden mind that s'much but then th' buggers took me smoothin' iyern en me dree castiyern saucepans s'well. Shan't never zee they agaane, dam th'ol 'Itler!"

J

Jackackter

If you are of a type who is devoted to presenting a public image of himself as being steeped in self-effacing ridicule, then you are a true *jackackter*. In an earlier age you might have won fame as a court jester. In North Cornwall, a district blessed with much more than its fair share of bona fide village idiots, it is often difficult to detect whether or not much of the *jackackter* behaviour seen taking place in the streets of villages like Port Isaac is contrived or genuine.

> *"Whabbee th' capital uv Cornwall?"*
> *"Ah do think tez Lundin!"*
> *"Caw buhy, you'm nart but a bleddy jackacter! Ev 'nother try."*
> *"P'raps tez th' letter C."*

In fond memory of Mrs Morman, second-class (seven to nine year olds) teacher at Port Isaac County Primary School.

Jacker

A native-born Cornishman blessed with having a shamelessly uncorrupted spoken accent. A *jacker's* family is able to trace its roots back into the mists of local history via countless generations of random inbreeding. A *jacker* who leaves Cornwall either willingly or as a result of forcible transportation to foreign parts at His or Her Majesty's pleasure is known by those among whom he then does dwell as a *Cousin Jack*.

> "Ah knawed ee wuz a jacker frum th' mineet ee did open yer gob. A jacker kin 'ide th' way a do zound a's r's, but when a do zay "reely" then tez a daid give 'way what a do be."

Jack's haass in Merrica

This is the time-honoured final resting place of anything or anyone which (or who) by accident or design is understood to be irretrievably lost, stolen, strayed or just plain gone away for ever.

> "Ah put me pint down, went t' git me darts, en come back t' vind me glaass 'ev bin empted. Where ev me beer gone to?"
>
> "Dun't ee worry buhy, a've gone up Jack's haass in Merrica."

Janner

A person cursed with the misfortune of being a native of the county located on the east bank of the River Tamar is a *janner*. Although in principle *janners* owe their allegiance to Devon, at a pinch an extension of the *janner* community into Somerset (where the cider apples are rumoured to grow) can also apply. The great regret of any *janner* is that he is not a *jacker* and neither can be or ever will be a *jacker*.

> "Ee kin truss a janner bout s'much as ee kin truss a taff, which reely edden nart 'tall. Other'n a cold shoulder, all they janners ev gived t' we jackers be Widdecombe fair t' zing bout. Janners do call a paasty a tetty oggie ef ee ever did ear anythin' s' maazed! A janner cooden maake a proper paasty any'ow t' saave a's life."

Jennelmin

Any male whose attributes include (inter alia) courtesy to others, politeness in company (mixed or otherwise) and close adherence to conventionally recognised standards of social etiquette is believed to be a *jennelmin*. His *modus operandi* is deference without compunction at all times to any female of the species, whom he will always consider to be a *laahduy*. In the streets of Port Isaac however, it is easier to find an impecunious farmer than it is to meet up with a *jennelmin* worthy of the accolade.

> *"Th' zahn 'bove th' doo-er do zay 'Jennelmin' but ah kin only s'pose that when ah zeed Jack en Les guyne in t' taake a piss they wooden much aable t' rayd. They doo buggers wooden spend a penny anyroad ayben ef they wuz bustin. Ef they'm jennelmin then zo be ah, en ah knaws full well that ah ben't."*

In fond memory of Messrs Jack McOwen and Les Honey of the Old Council Houses

Jerry

As a receptacle traditionally fashioned in vitreous china, a *jerry* is frequently decorated with a floral transfer on both its exterior and its rather more important interior. A *jerry* looks like an exceedingly large round cup with an appropriately sized handle to match. Also known as a *po* or a *piss-pot*, the normal resting place of a *jerry* in the cottage is under a bed within easy reach of the bed's occupant(s), so that it can be withdrawn in an instant to receive the voided fruits of nocturnal calls of nature. The volume capacity of a *jerry* is normally sufficient to avoid any possibility of its overflowing before dawn—its accumulated contents are discharged in the great outdoors when morning eventually gilds the skies.

> *"Mother, there do be zum gipsies comin' up th' road en they dun't look t' be up t' no good!"*

"Ayve th' upstairs winda open maid, en empt the jerry out over the buggers, tez still vull frum las' night!"

Jew

One who has a talent to *jew* possesses an instinctive skill that allows him to obtain an advantage over others that is likely to be to his financial gain. While the act of *jewin* is not exactly illegal, anyone who has been *jewed* is sure to complain of being the victim of sharp practice.

> *"Ah went t' th' fruiterer downtown t' git me zwayte rashin, en do ee knaw buhy, th' miser'ble bugger broke up a biled bit uv barley sugar to jew me out uv evin a skerrick moo-er than me doo ounsis."*
>
> *"Aiz buhy, Ah've zeed un at ut. Las week a jew'd me fer aff uv a apple, en ah still ad t' pay un fer ut!"*

In fond memory of Mr Altair "no tick here" Bunt of the Pentice

Jip

To all intents and purposes, the verbs to *jip* and to *jew* more or less mean the same thing. For anyone who has been subjected to the art of *jippin* however, the consequences of a good *jip* are considered to be ever so slightly more benign than those that come from being *jewed*.

> *"Ah dedden want t' buy no onions frum th' Frenchmin when a come long on a's bike, but a edden zich a bad ol' buhy reely zo ah 'ad t' git a stringuv em off uv un. Tez a bit uv a jip fer me coorse, but ah dun't mind so much when tez zumwan like that bugger who do be jippin me."*

Jouder

An itinerant vendor of the fruits of the sea, a *jouder* (more completely referred to as a **vish jouder**) plys his trade around the St

Endellion parish and some parts of the adjoining districts beyond in a motorised van, from the back of which he purveys a variety of species of dead fish and (possibly) live crustaceans of indifferent quality to a rural clientele. Needless to add, but it ought to be added anyway, a well-established *jouder* and the practices of both *jippin* and *jewin* do not make strange bedfellows.

> *Dicky Dido jouds vish,*
> *Penny-ayp'ny a dish!*
> *Dun't ee buy em!*
> *Dun't ee buy em!*
> *They do stink when ee do fry em!*

In fond memory of Mr Tony "Bollicks" Robinson of Fore Street

Jowds

Jowds are the myriad pieces into which a brittle artefact gets shattered on making sudden contact with a solid stationary feature on which it may have been dropped or at which it could equally in the Port Isaac context have been aggressively thrown. The end result is the same whether or not the breakage into *jowds* was effected by accident, in jest, through anger or as part of a grand design.

> "When 'Arry come 'ome aff cut frum th' pub, a's missis ayved wan uv er bes' plaates at un, en caitched th' ol' bugger vull on th' aid. The pity uv ut wuz that th' plaate wuz all scat t' jowds while 'Arry dedden ayben git a scraitch."

In fond memory of Mr Harry "Bluff" May of Hartland Road

Jussnow

As far as carrying out an action in a timely manner is concerned, doing it *jussnow* ranks it as being perhaps a little more likely to be done than its famous sister qualification **dreckly** is understood to imply. On the other hand, all things are relative in Port Isaac, where the principle that one should never do today what can be put aside for doing tomorrow always takes precedence where work is concerned.

"Ow long do ee think twill be afower you'm reddy t' cut me air?"

"Dun't ee worry buhy, ah'll be gittin' to ee jussnow!"

"Thass awright then! There do be time fer me t' git off t' zee t' me gardin en pull a couple raw uv tetties fust."

K

Kaype

When you *kaype* something you normally reckon it to be your personal property. You may have acquired what you have in hand to *kaype* through purchase—equally it may have come to you as a gift or even as a Sunday school prize. Alternatively you might have *jewed* or *jipped* someone out of it, or picked it up purely by chancing on it lying around in keeping with that time-honoured expression *vahnders, kaypers.* A good Port Isaac man doesn't care where a thing comes from—whatever he can get hold of by whatever means, he is ready to take it all home to *kaype* for his own. An alternative meaning for *kaype* is applied to a popular activity in which a fisherman's punt is cared for in and around the harbour by a group of boys while the fisherman is out to sea about his business. This activity is known as *kaypin*—the boys *kaype* the punt without actually owning it.

> "Do ee think th' p'leeceman do kaype what gits 'anded inta th' staashin be they 'oo d' vahnd th' things en 'oo be too bleddy maazed t'kaype em fer theirzelfs?"
>
> "That p'leecman! Th' bugger cooden kaype a's 'elmit on ef a wooden told be zumwan what a's aid be fer!"

116

Koo

A long and invariably slow-moving single-file column of people, chiefly females. The individuals who form a *koo* tend to shuffle along with glum expressions on their faces as the *koo* advances. Everyone in a *koo* is intent on obtaining a share (which under no circumstances will ever be considered by them to be a fair share) of whatever commercial wares are available up at the *koo's* head by the time they get there and have their turn.

> "*Me zister wuz in th' koo fer they bananas down be th' greengrocer's fer dree hour, en when er comed up front all er wuz gived be Jim May wuz wan banana. Er zayed twuz all wuth th'effert though—twuz the fust banana er'd zeed zince th' war started, en er wuz zet on gittin' 'old uv wan be 'ook er be crook.*"

In fond memory of Mr Jim "the ice cream man" May of Victoria House, lower Fore Street

L

Laacin

This a euphemism for both the most popular (with certain teachers) form of corporal punishment administered to pupils at the school and also for the tried and true home-based type of chastisement afflicted on most younger members of the family. *Laacin* requires a thin whippy stick or a custom-made bamboo cane for use as its key tool. The *laacin* technique gets its name from the intricate pattern of wheals that an expert in the art of wielding the stick is able to lay out on the skin of his victim. Alternatives to *laacin* as a means of defining the variety of approaches with which a Port Isaac boy expects to be castigated are *ammerin, draishin, baytin, larrupin, caanin, lickin, whippin, scattin*—the list is long. Foreign observers have questioned how it can be that in a village in which few of the resident population are overtaxed by any breadth of vocabulary there can be so many words referring to corporal punishment? The answer is, why not? After all, Eskimos have innumerable words to describe snow.

"Tez ayther that ah do be a reely baad bugger, er else th' aidmaaster dun't like me atall, cuz dun't matter what ah d'

do, a alwys zeem t' want t' pull me out up front uv th' claass fer a laacin'. Ah s'pose tez all me awn vault—faather d' zay taychurs do be alwys in th'right. All th' saame, wan day ah shall be s' gurt as th' aidmaaster do be now, then us'll zee 'oo gits t' laace 'oo!"

In memory of Mr Henry "The Eighth" Pam, dictatorial master of the third class (nine to eleven year olds) at Port Isaac County Primary School

Laake

The cleansing stream of water that clinks and bubbles down to the Port Isaac beach from its source in the first folds of the sweet valley of the parish hinterland is known throughout its masonry-contained course alongside Middle Street as the *Laake*. As a depository for much downtown household refuse of the organic variety, the *Laake* is equipped at its upstream head-point with a transverse flush gate, which when shut is able to pen up a mighty volume of incoming water. On release of the flush gate a veritable tidal wave is then induced to rush down along the *Laake* to the beach, where it expends its fury and delights the gulls with the scoured-out cargo of edible treats it brings to them.

"When th' Laake flush be reddy, a ole ayp uv buhys do be there waitin' fer un to lift. After ol' Ned ayves up th' bar en the gaate laypes open, we raaces th' gurt waave down t' th' baych, coosin s'ard ez we kin 'long Middle Strayte. The bleddy waave do alwys git t' th' baych afower we buhys though."

In fond memory of Mr Ned Cowlyn of Church Hill

Laig

The name of each of a pair of lengthy appendages which taken in concert form the lower portion of the human anatomy. One of these is identified as the *lef' laig* and the other is called the *ryte laig*. A not insignificant proportion of Port Isaac people, especially boys, are allegedly unable to distinguish the one from the other. A typical *laig* commences at the pendant of a backside (*haass*) cheek; heads downwards via a thigh (*theye*); bends more or less at the half-way point in a knee (*nay*—the plural being *naze*); descends onwards through a calf (*caff*); and terminates in a foot (*voot*—plural *vit*). *Laigs* are vital personal attributes for maintaining the good order of walking and/or running, and it will probably be obvious to readers that anyone who has only one *laig* (or less) would be unable to participate in a *haass-kickin* contest.

> *Bollicks Bill*
> *Went up th' 'ill,*
> *T' 'ev a gaame uv cricket.*
> *Th' ball went up*
> *A's trowser laig*
> *En 'it a's middle wicket!*

In fond memory of Mr Raymond "Ido" Glover of Hartland Road

Langwidge

Langwidge is the type of English spoken by the *Likes uv They*. Examples of this are found in the mellifluously plummy announcer-cum-newsreader tones heard on the BBC Home Service; the unpleasantly brittle twittering voices of persons who allegedly have blue blood running in their veins; and certain of the impenetrable and ear-jarring accents that fight their way into Cornwall from provincial locations somewhere *up th' line*. Port Isaac people are never absolutely certain if what they speak is or is not a Cornish variant of *langwidge*, but it matters not as they don't give a shite one way or the other. When, as they so often do, the *Likes uv They* disparage the sounds marking the way in which Port Isaac people converse, the former soon discover that the latter are as adept as they are in the use of what is known as *baad langwidge.*

> *"Taake ol' Spokeshaave now, they do zay a wuz a gurt
> maaster fer langwidge. 'T' be er not t' be, that do be the
> kweschin', wuz a faamuss zayin that a did come up with."*

> *"Aiz, ah ad t' rayd frum Omellit's surlillerkwee down be th'
> skool, en all ah could think uv when ah wuz raydin uv ut wuz
> what th' bleddy 'ell do ut all mayne?"*

Lanson Jail

Any place said to look like *Lanson Jail* is by definition invested with
a state of untidiness that is not only the epitome of rank disorder
but also characterised by an all too evident lack of attention to
the maintenance of acceptable standards of hygiene. The place of
incarceration in the town of *Lanson* (written as "Launceston" on
official maps) which motivated the absolutely legendary *Lanson Jail*
sentiment is now defunct. In its heyday the said prison was no doubt
established to provide for the enduring discomfort of its inmates.
Lanson, located in North-east Cornwall, was the county's capital
prior to that distinction being reassigned to Bodmin in a politically
inspired move implying that a looney bin confers more status on a
town than does a jail. Of course, Bodmin had a jail as well, but it
presumably didn't compare with the *Lanson* version. It is sometimes
permissible for *Baul Councilouses* to be substituted for *Lanson Jail*
in conversation in accordance with judgement and taste. Residents
of the Baul council houses near Wadebridge were reputed to chop
up doors, banisters and other wooden fittings of their homes for use
as kindling for the fireplace and in addition to have *hunderds* of coal
dumped for storage in their bathtubs. A further option to describe a
Lanson Jail type of community dysfunction is *Troy Town,* borrowed
from the celebrated novel of the same name by Sir Arthur Quiller-
Couch.

"Twuz our turn this 'ear t' clayne op th' Church Rooms after the Zundy skool Chrissmuss party. Caw, what a job! Twuz lookin like Lanson Jail afower they little buggers all went 'ome!"

Larrups

The loose folds of several sizes too large clothes hanging on a Port Isaac boy's undersized frame are called *larrups*. The mismatch (and mish-mash) of fit is a function of uninspired parental judgement at the moment of purchase. Hand-me-downs from an elder sibling can have precisely the same *larrups*-generating effect, however.

"'Ere buhy, try on yer noo grammer skool oonyform so us kin zee what ut do look like on ee!"

"Lookit me, mother, Ah told ee twuz a ole ayp too big fer me, tez all angin' off me in gurt larrups!"

"Never do ee mind buhy, ee'll graw into un in a'ear er doo!"

Layve

This word has two important meanings—which are not unrelated:
(1) you *layve* someone or something when you permit or allow him or her or it, without any compunction whatsoever on your part and as often as not with an unwarranted flush of personal confidence that all will subsequently be well, to remain just where he or she or it is actually located at that particular moment
(2) you *layve* somewhere when you depart from it with the intention of proceeding to somewhere else. Any Port Isaac workman likes to think that he can *layve* his place of work through a figurative front door, but he is usually shown the tradesman's way out when the *Likes uv They* direct his egress.

"Ol' man Button did near nuff caitch we scrumpin' apples in

122

a's archerd. Us 'ad t' drop en layve on th' ground all th' apples
we 'ad, en t' layve the plaace ourzelfs out over the barb wire.
T'wooden aizy, but us did git 'way, though ah tored the haass
out uv me trowsis guyne over th' bleddy wire!"

In fond memory of Mr Button of Tregaverne Farm

Lard

If the *Lard* did not actually exist, it is claimed by those who say
they know him that he would have to have been invented. He is
worshipped by Church and Chapel people alike, although whether
or not not the sincerity of all such worshippers is to be believed may
be open to debate. The *Lard* shares his title with the deathly (and
deadly) white fat that Granny Spry once used (over and over again)
in the big fryer in her chip shop in Middle Street. The fact that there
are two *lards* may confuse the uninitiated, but given the choice in
Port Isaac between a chip or a church related variety of *lard* it will
always be clear which of the two enriches life best in the here and
now and which one doesn't.

> *The Lard zayed unta Moses,*
> *"All men shall ev long noses—*
> *Cep' fer yer brother Aaron,*
> *A's guyne ev a square un!"*

And in another playground gem:

> *The Lard zayed unta Moses,*
> *"Come forth!"*
> *But Moses come fifth,*
> *En a lost a's beer munny.*

Lecktricks

Emanating as if by magic from a source referred to by the

grandiloquent title of "the Mains", *lecktricks* are conducted into both domestic and commercial premises via an array of rubber-coated copper wires which terminate (in relative security) in what are spoken of as power points. *Lectricks* cannot be seen, smelt or heard—if they are touched or tasted however, as for example by a small boy inserting an index finger or perhaps even sticking his tongue into a power point socket hole, the sensation of liberated power that the small boy receives in return will be as sudden as it is shocking. The technicalities of what *lectricks* consist of is not a topic of conversation heard much in the streets of Port Isaac. It is enough for the general public to know that *lectricks* exist and are there to serve it, to the extent that by merely flicking a switch and declaring "Let there be light", there will be light in the cottage and lo one can see it, that it is good.

> *"They do ev th' lectricks in alreddy up be th' top uv th' village. Ol' mother Smith tol' me bout ut. Er've got em in, but 'er dun't do nart with em cuz 'er zayed er do prefer usin' ile lamps t' zee en th' vire fer cookin' er dinner. Ef God wantid 'er t' bugger round with lectricks er zayed, a would ev rote 'bout em in the Bahbull, en a dedden do that! Coorse, er can't rayd, zo 'ow would 'er knaw what God rit?"*

Lettinoff

This is the perenially popular act in which you void intestinal wind, whether or not you do it inadvertently or (better yet) deliberately. In all instances of *lettinoff* the time-honoured adage "better out than in" will apply. *Lettinoff* ideally produces a staccato ripple of sound coupled to perfection with an evil pungency of smell that Port Isaac boys find highly entertaining, especially when the smell breaks out in mixed company and the identity of the perpetrator is unknown. It is, however, in an ability for *lettinoff* silently that the process is raised to fine art status—such surreptitious blasts of wind take no

124

prisoners and never reveal the *haass* of origin.

> *"What do travel faastest, wind er zound?"*
> *"I do think tez zound!"*
> *"No buhy, th' anser do be wind, cuz no zooner do a good*
> *lettinoff layve yer haass than a's up yer nose fer shelter!"*

Or, with grateful thanks to an anonymous poet who once frequented the *Jennelmins* section of the Port Isaac public lavatory with time on both of his hands, a pencil in his pocket and a convenient patch of wall to write on:

> *Ah dedden come 'ere t' spit en coff,*
> *Jus' wanted t' shit then bugger off.*
> *Now 'ere ah zits with broken 'art,*
> *Ah spent me penny en kin only fart.*
>
> *Tez a zad deelemmer with which ah do wrassle,*
> *Ah ebben got a dree-speed haassawl.*
> *But ef ah 'ad, wan thing d'be clear,*
> *Ah could be lettinoff in low gear.*

And finally, as Mr Tom Brown was wont to put it so succinctly to the many boys who admired him so much:

> *"Ev ee ever 'eard yer bum go boom?"*

Liard

A person widely recognised as accomplished in dispensing the truth with an impressive amount of economy is a *liard*. In the type of society favoured by the the *Likes uv They*, a *liard* is sometimes referred to as a "bullshit artist".

> *"Gaggy tol' we there wuz a foo nice bits uv wreck waished*
> *up on the baych down be Varley Zands. Us did maycase*
> *downalong there t' git 'em, but there wooden nart zee on*

*th' baych 'tall. Ah should've knawn t'would be like that, ol'
Gaggy bein' zich a liard."*

In fond memory of Mr William "Gaggy" Hosking of Fore Street, Roscarrock
Hill and China Downs

Likes

Likes embodies the perfect blend of spiritual, cultural, social and
moral compass that defines the quality of a rural community united
by blood ties into a tribalistic bond. Herd-type behaviour is one
of its principal characteristics. By Port Isaac convention, society is
subdivided into a poverty-wracked majority known as the *Likes
uv We*; and a wealthy minority called the *Likes uv They*. The *Likes
uv We*, born to serve the *Likes uv They* with forelock-touching
deference, are sustained by deep local taproots put down over many
generations. The *Likes uv They* originate almost entirely from
foreign stock and have come to reserve their right to rule, govern,
exploit and in every way behave as if they were superior to the *Likes
uv We*. In doing so, the *Likes uv They* demonstrate that although
their money bought them an expensive education it didn't purchase
them too much intelligence.

> *"Gran, ah do wonder ef ah shall drahve a gurt ol' car en live
> in a big 'ouse with a ayp uv sarvints when ah graws up?"*
>
> *"Dun't ee git too many uv they idees 'bove yer staashun
> me 'ansum, tedden fer th' Likes uv We t' want t' live like our
> betters. Th' Likes uv They knaws whass bes' fer We en t'wunt
> do ee no good t' think otherwise!"*

In loving memory of Mrs Eleanor "Gran" Creighton of Canadian Terrace

Longaided

A well-read person with a keenly-honed intellect, whose breadth of
general knowledge is never hidden like a light left under a bushel and

for whom humility counts for just about bugger all, is considered to be a *longaided* type. Port Isaac natives fully accept a *longaided* condition in one of the *Likes uv They* but frown on its manifestation in one of their own, not least when palpable airs, graces and expressions of what are known as *zide* are also in evidence.

> *"Ah dun't never rayd they books what ebben got big rytin en ayps uv peckchurs in em! Books that do be all paages uv small rytin do be fair nuff fer zum longaided bugger t' shove a's nose inta, but fer me all they'm good fer be lightin' vires, maakin fag paapers, en wipin' yer haass on."*

Lopster

A fearsome looking dark blue-coloured marine crustacean equipped with eight legs, two highly threatening claws, a hard yet articulate armoured carapace and a constantly questing pair of long orange antennae. Much prized for its flesh by the gentry and others of the *Likes uv They* ilk who possess more money than sense, *lopsters* are trapped on the sea bed in an ingenious contraption known as a *lopster* (or crab) pot which was manually woven from cut withies before being taken out to sea in a fishing boat to be dropped at its place of work. As a precursor to its flesh being eaten a *lopster* is boiled alive, in which process its colour is transformed to bright red—and who on earth can blame it for that?

> *"Tom, why do ee pack they lopsters up with all that zawdust in th' boxes afore ee do zend em t' th'train staashun?"*
> *"Well me buhys, zince ee all do ask, ah be guyne tell ee! Tez cuz they lopsters loves t'ayt th' ol' sawdust 'long th' way. Then when they gits t' where they'm guyne to they shits out planks that kin be zawed up t' maake moo-er boxes en a good ayp uv zawdust fer the nex' shipmint!"*

With many thanks to the incomparable Mr Tom Brown, Manager of Pawlyn's Cellars

And if Tom's story isn't true, then it **bleddy** well ought to be!

Box be open.
Lopster in.
Zawdust on top,
Close agin.

Lopster d'like zawdust.
Lopster d'give thanks.
Lopster d'ayt zawdust.
Lopster d'shit planks.

Planks be took out.
Planks be zawed.
Piles uv zawdust,
Ayps uv boo-ard.

Boo-ards maakes boxes.
Lopster in.
Zawdust cover.
Start agin.

Claws is nicked.
Lopster ken't bite 'ee.
So ut goes.
Deer God Almighty!

A tribute to Mr Tom Brown

Lousterin

The performance of the type of work which calls for much physical effort and the not infrequent use of a long-handled shovel to move loose material from one location to another (and maybe even back again) is termed *lousterin*. The beauty of a long-handled shovel to a Port Isaac workman is that it can be planted vertically in the ground so as to be leaned on in comfort whenever the foreman isn't around.

> *"Ol' 'Arry Bluff wuz gived a job lousterin down be th' clay
> works. Musta bin th' fust job that laazy bugger ad in 'ears, en
> a juss laastid a day at ut. Twuz zaid down pub that th' doctor
> be guyne zend Arry t'osspittle fer a x-ray t' zee ef they kin
> vind any work in 'un anywhere."*

With many thanks to the ever genial Mr Fred Ball of lower Dolphin Street

Lurgy

A malaise of convenience for all seasons, *lurgy* may be visited upon
anyone who is suddenly confronted with a requirement to perform
a task or duty that he or she would rather avoid doing altogether.
The condition can be quite contagious when symptoms such as
reluctance to attend school; facing up to *lousterin* or visiting the
dentist enter the equation.

> *"Ee kin alwys tell when tez gittin time fer th' dree hour long
> Good Vrahdy affnoon sarvice down church, cuz aff th' buhys
> in th' choir goes down with lurgy in th' marnin! Still, never do
> ee mind, they'm all better gaane be aybenin."*

129

M

Maaster

An admirable quality possessed by someone or alternatively something that can be acceptably compared with the biggest and best of his, her or its kind, whatever and wherever it happens to be encountered.

> *"This spring there do be a maaster gurt shaw uv primrosies down be Pine Awn. Ah ebben never zeed th' likes afower. Tez a maaster zight ah kin tell 'ee."*

Maazed

By popular consensus, *maazed* is the alleged state of mind of someone whose behaviour and demeanour are reckoned to diverge far enough from Port Isaac standards of the same (in all their wild diversity) to allow him or her to be spoken of in terms of one or more of the following—being a corner short of a pasty; having one claw less than a lobster; being subject to a screw coming loose upstairs; being afflicted with bats in the belfry; being nuttier than a hazel tree in autumn; and, in what perhaps reaches the absolute pinnacle of acclaim, belonging in Bodmin. The nature of being *maazed* is honoured in a classic simile in association with the well-known floor sweeping implement that Mr Fuller's representatives travel around the parish and go from door to door with in a vain attempt to sell it to residents within.

> *"Cap'n, ah be zorry ah did zay 'ee wuz s' maazed ez a brish,*
> *en then go on t' tell they buhys that ee d' belong in Bommin."*
> *"Ah do be glad t' 'ear ut buhy, en from now on when ah*
> *maakes yer tay ah ben't guyne piss in th' taypot no moo-er!"*

In affectionate memory of Mr Leonard "Cockeye" Mitchell of Hartland Road

Maid

The feminine equivalent of *buhy*, *maid* is an affectionate title given to a girl whose age may be anywhere from babe in arms up to school leaving. *Maid* can also also be used as a term of familiarity by which a married woman is addressed by her peers—although a young woman of marriageable age is more likely to be spoken of as a *maiden*. It is considered dangerous for you to refer to any dyed-in-the-wool spinster of St Endellion parish as *maid* within her audible range however, not least if she appears to be holding a walking stick and is standing within easy striking distance of you.

> *"Ah do tell ee maid, that maiden uv mine ev got no idee 'bout*
> *'ow t' crimp a paasty. Er do go at the paastry like a cow 'andlin*
> *a musket."*

Mangull

A *mangull*, or to give it its extended name a *mangull-wurzle*, is a commercially grown root vegetable which looks rather like an extra-large yellowish turnip. *Mangulls* are harvested in the late autumn of each year by the farmers who cultivate them and are then stored away in bulk to provide a ready source of winter feed for farm livestock. Yet as all good Port Isaac boys know, the manifest destiny of a prime *mangull* is to be lifted clandestinely from its field of origin in early November and from thence to be taken home for topping, tailing and washing clean of soil before being carefully hollowed out. Thereafter, following the excision of a few holes cleverly arranged to simulate facial features in the *mangull's* shell and the placement of a candle in the hollow, a lantern to grace **Guy Fox** night is born. The flesh of a *mangull* is very much to the taste of cattle, but it is not recommended for consumption by boys, as any boy who has tried it out will know only too well.

> *"Sam Blaake ev got zome maaster mangulls in a's vield up 'bove Seb'm Aacres. Us kin aizy git over th' ol' ayge down on th' valley zide t' lift a foo uv em, en ol' Sam wun't never knaw th' differnce."*

In fond memory of Mr Sam Blake of Trewetha Farm

Marnin

The portion of a day (any day will do) which commences from the moment when the sun rises in the east (its visibility dependent on cloud cover) and the stroke of noon (when *dinner* goes on the table).

> *"Good marnin buhy!"*
> *"Whass good 'bout ut? Tez emptin' down outzide!"*

Mary

A less than flattering categorisation of a male (man or boy) who in the view of his peers exhibits those so-called *zoft-ez-shit* mannerisms that seem to be as neat and clean in character as they are stylish in execution. A *Mary* has a strong tendency to participate in practices, activities and home-based hobbies that are normally associated with feminine wiles.

132

"Taake they dree Smith buhys now. Stanley en Charlie, they'm jus' s' ard ez nails, but as fer th' t'other, well a do be a proper Mary."

In fond memory once again of Mr and Mrs Smith's three not-so-little boys.

Mawn

Also referred to as a *pad*, a *mawn* is a large round basket manually woven from withies in the shape of an inverted truncated cone that is almost as broad as it is deep. A stout pair of diametrically opposed handles, also fashioned from withies, are added to a *mawn* to embellish its upper rim, reflecting the fact that once it is fully loaded, transporting a *mawn* is very much a two-man carrying job. A *mawn* is employed to transport the fish and marine crustaceans caught by boats of the Port Isaac fishing fleet from their harbour moorings up to Pawlyn's fish cellars at the head of the Town Platt beside the lifeboat slipway—and then to bring fishermen's paraphernalia back down to the boats on the return journey.

"Ow did th' errin vishin go las' night?"
"T'wooden bad buhy. Us brought in nuff vish t' vill den mawn, though wan mawn den times'd be more like ut, cuz we only do ev wan uv they buggers."

Maycase

An instruction to a laggard, usually made not without a degree of emotion by one of his (or her) elders and betters in order to induce him (or her) to carry out a required task by demonstrating a lot more despatch and willingness than he (or she) has been showing thus far.

"Maycase en git yer boots on er ee'll be laate fer skool agaane! You'm alwys ome on the dot fer dinner time, so why ken't ee move a bit vaaster guyne t'other way?"

Mayt

Mayt, customarily purchased from a butcher, is an essential ingredient in the preparation of most of the dinners that appear on the table during the week. On Saturday mornings it is a Port Isaac family routine to send its least willing member up to the butcher to obtain a sufficiently large piece of **mayt** (technically known as a *jynt*) to furnish not only the basis for dinner on the morrow but also to provide left-overs to contribute to dinner time on Monday and most likely on Tuesday as well. The usual type of **mayt** available on the butcher's block is called **bayf,** although with a stroke of luck a piece of **lam** or even **park** can turn up sometimes. When **mayt** is in short supply (perish the thought) the butcher is likely to offer alternatives referred to collectively as **awful** or **innerds**—these include **art,** the appropriately named **tripe,** and **levver.** One of the blessings of a good **paasty** is that it makes a little **mayt** go a long way.

> *"That bit uv mayt us ad fer las' Zundy dinner, caw twus s' rough ez Roughtor! Valse teeth cooden maneege ut! Ah could ev stuck ut t' th' zoles uv me vit with tar and walked on ut t' Waybridge en back en still t'wooden uv bin tender."*

In fond memory of the master butcher and pillar of St Peter's church Mr Westlake Brown of Rose Hill

Mind

A selective memory-filtering ploy instinctively used by many miserable old buggers when they recall (over and over again) how much better things were during the time of their youth. *Aiz,* they will tell you, they **mind** when an orange could be bought for a ha'penny (or stolen for nothing) and be peeled and eaten while they sat in a tin bath of lukewarm water for their once-weekly ablutions in front of the kitchen fire with a bar of carbolic soap calling vainly for their attention on one side.

"Ah do mind th' time when ah wuz guyne skool, en 'ow ef ah did look zideways at th' taychur a would knock me down with a good ol' clout round me aid. They skooldays wuz th' 'appiest days uv me life!"

In fond memory of Mr Freddie Honey, Liberal Club custodian in Fore Street

Mineet

A period of time consisting of exactly sixty seconds, of which there are coincidentally sixty such periods making up every single hour of every day. In spite of such a quantification however, a *mineet* passed pleasurably always seems to vanish a lot more rapidly than does a *mineet* spent undertaking onerous duties. Sitting in church with a sermon droning in your ears can make a *mineet* feel as long as an hour. A *mineet* can additionally assume a fair amount of elasticity, as anyone who has been asked to wait for one of the same or whose performance has been judged on the experience of five of them will be quick to admit.

"Jus' a mineet, where be that fowntin pen ee wuz gived fer yer las' birfdy?
"Ah los' un, didden ah!"
"Los' un? Ee only got un dree munce back! Ee ken't never kip nart fer moo-er'n vahve mineets!"

Minjee

A *minjee* person is one who lacks charity, with faith and hope being also qualities he exhibits in short supply. The diagnostic feature of *minjeeniss* is a compulsive reluctance to part with money. For that matter, anything of any kind whatsoever that a *minjee* type hands over to others is doled out sparingly as a rule, and invariably carries a sting in its tail. Naturally enough you can only be *minjee* if you

135

have money in your pocket to start with, and that proviso at once eliminates far too many Port Isaac folk from judgement.

> *"That bugger do be s' minjee that ef a wuz t' shit in yer gardin a would skin the turds off so ez not t' let ee ev all uv em."*

Miser'ble

A way of life that is especially well-developed in those who have recognisably reached the more advanced years of life. It is generally accepted that men are more prone to be *miser'ble* than are women, yet in Port Isaac many elderly females are by no means exempt from the condition. The symptoms of being *miser'ble* include a display of elements of some (or all) of the following: bad temper, argumentativeness, intolerance (especially of boys and their ways), parsimony, self-importance, sanctimony, meanness of spirit—well, you must have got the picture by now. Both Church and Chapel congregations are well able to claim more than their fair share of *miser'ble* old buggers, but the greater of these is Chapel.

> *"Jack Shite do be the most miser'ble ol' bugger ah knaws. A would cross the strayte t' gob bacca joose on ee sooner'n do ee a faaver."*

In fond memory of Mr Jack Short and his wife Mrs Phoebe Short of upper Dolphin Street

Morra

Morra is what today was said to be when it was looked at from the vantage point of yesterday.

> *"Zum bugger zayed morra be guyne be 'nother day, but then zum other bugger zayed morra dun't never come, zo ah dun't knaw what t' bleeve."*

136

Munce

The *munce* (singular *munf*) of the year are twelve in number, each consisting of a numerically distinctive succession of days. Not every one of the sequence of *munce* contains the same number of given days as its predecessor, but not to worry, it all sorts itself out in the end, allowing an orderly sequence of the twelve to cumulate into three hundred and sixty-five days for three years out of four, with the fourth (known as a *laype 'ear*) having three hundred and sixty-six days.

The conventional names of the twelve *munce* in sequence from the start through to the finish of a year is as follows:
Jannery, Feberry, March, Aaperl, May, Joon, J'ly, Awguss, Siptemmer, October, Novemmer, Dissemmer.

> *"Th' bes' uv all th' munce be Awguss when us ev's th' long skool ollydays ah do s'pose, though ah do deerly like Dissemmer s'well, cuz thass when tez Chrissmuss."*

Munny

A commodity that allegedly makes the world go round, but which curiously enough is also said to be the root of all evil. To its credit however, *munny* not only keeps the wolf from the door but also (when handed over to a third party in the desired amount) permits the same door when opened to mollify the ire of the rent man when he comes knocking. Whether or not *munny* can buy happiness is a moot question that can only be answered by those who have plenty of it to be *minjee* with.

For the record, the various denominations of *munny* in circulation in Port Isaac are (set against their comparative values) as follows:

Coins
Farthin' (copper)   One quarter of a penny
Ayp'ny (copper)   One half of a penny

Penny or *copper* (copper)	One whole penny (what else!)
Drepny bit (silver, and rare)	Three pence
Drepny bit (brass)	Three pence
Tanner (silver)	Six pence
Bob (silver)	Twelve pence (one shilling)
Florin (silver)	Two shillings
'Aff crown (silver)	Two shillings and six pence
Crown or **vahve bob** (silver commemorative)	Five shillings

Paper

Denbobnote (brown engraved)	Ten shillings
Pounnote (green engraved)	One pound or twenty shillings
Vahvepounnote (black on white)	Five pounds or one hundred shillings

The probability of a Port Isaac shopper being able to produce any of the listed denominations of *munny* from his or her pocket or purse decreases in direct proportion to the value of the denomination. The presentation of a *vahvepounnote* to a shopkeeper would be viewed by the latter with the utmost suspicion coupled with immediate thoughts of sending for the policeman.

Occasionally a Lundy Island penny known as a *puffin* turns up in shop change. Here's richness!

> *Munny do be the root uv all ayvul!*
> *Munny do be the root uv all ayvul!*
> *Munny do be the root uv all ayvul!*
> *Bring ut 'ere!*
> *Bring ut 'ere!*
> *Bring ut 'ere!*

In fond memory of Mrs Alice Keat of lower Front Hill

Murr

A name shared by the two most common species of auk, specifically the razorbill and the guillemot, that frequent the cliffs at Welshman's Quarry and Bounds Cliff up to the east of Port Gaverne during the bird's-egging season. A third species of auk, the highly distinctive puffin, is of such rarity around the coast of Port Isaac Bay that it is allowed to retain its proper name.

A few other familiar names by which some well-known birds are referred to by Port Isaac boys are as follows:

Aygee	Hedge sparrow (hedge accentor)
Black Annie	Greater black-backed gull
Blackie	Blackbird
Chaaf	Cornish chough
Fuzz Jack	Chaffinch
Jan Dawe	Jackdaw
Maggie	Magpie
Rennie	Wren
Shank	Shag
Songie	Song thrush
Towncraw	Carrion crow
Water hen	Moorhen
Walter wagtail	Pied wagtail

"*Th' trubble with murrs do be that they lays their aigs be narra layges that do be s' diffycult to climb up t'. But ef ee kin git be 'em then tez wuth ut, cuz th' aigs do be big en shaaped like cones with good markins en luv'ly colours, speshly th' grayne wans.*"

N

Nart

Nart means nothing. *Nart* is zero. In fact, *nart* is bugger all. You can make your choice as to which of the foregoing you prefer. However much *nart* may be equal to nothing at all however, the word *art* does not exist as a positive means of specifying something—unless the organ in your chest pumping blood around your body is taken into consideration.

> *"Wuzzee wan uv they buhys what locked ol' Jack Shite up in a's celler esterdy en ayved 'way the kay?"*
> *"Naw ah wooden! Ah dedden do nart uv ut, though zince twuz Jack Shite that wuz shut in ah do deerly wish ah'd uv bin the wan what done uv ut!"*

Naw

The almost inevitably negative response that is emitted by anyone asked to fulfil a request, a demand or a command that he is reluctant to comply with. *Naw* is sometimes (although not always given the dire state of polite etiquette that exists in Port Isaac), made palatable by coupling it to an expression of thanks. An alternative means of expressing a feeling of negativity is to use an aspirate *ho*. This finds its place chiefly with people such as fishermen who favour economy of speech.

> "Wooden ee like t' go down t' th' chelderns soshull be th' Temprince 'All s'aybenin?"
> "Naw thanks faather! I zees all they buggers oo be guyne ever' day down be th' skool, en thass moo-er'n nuff fer me!"

Nayder

A word inserted into a conversation in order to leave a listener in absolutely no doubt that in a situation for which two dubious courses of action are feasible, both can be rejected with confidence on grounds of not being worth the effort. *Nayder* is always employed in association with its close cousin *ner*—the shortfall on choice is then conventionally expressed as *"nayder th' wan ner th' t'other"*.

> *Ee do zay either en ah do zay ayder;*
> *Ee do zay neither en ah do zay nayder—*
> *Either, ayder,*
> *Neither, nayder,*
> *Less call th'ole thing off!*

With thanks to Mr George Gershwin

Nice-gutted

An accusation likely to be levelled at anyone whose culinary tastes transcend the limitations of the **dinner time** fare selection at home. In declining to consume certain of mother's plated-up offerings a *nice-gutted* diner becomes the complete antithesis of one whose *"eyes do be bigger than a's belly"*. The *nice-gutted* crave to divorce themselves from the society of the bland eating the bland in favour of consummating a relationship with **boughten** food in dining establishments open to non-residents, in which the varied menu of the day supplants the home-based constraint of Hobson's choice.

> "*Ee ebben ayted op moo-er'n a skerrick uv yer tetty uddle! Tedden good nuff! Ever since ee went out t' ev yer dinner up be Pendogget pub las' wayke, ee do be too nice-gutted fer yer awn good!*"

Nickin

A traditional fisherman's practice in which a well-whetted clasp knife blade is applied to the job of slitting the tough tendon-like membranes on the great claws of both crabs and lobsters. The objective of *nickin* is to completely eliminate the danger posed by the active claws of these live shellfish to fishermen, fish *jouders* (not that too many people are inclined to worry about the safety of a fish *jouder's* fingers) and members of the general public who are their customers.

> "*Ol' Nibs ev bin nickin' waiters fer donkeys' 'ears, but a missed wan claw a fortnight back, en th' bleddy crab took off the top jynt uv a's middle vinger in th' blink uv a eye.*"

In fond memory of Mr Frank "Nibs" Brown of upper Fore Street

Noo

As applied to material possessions, *noo* is the opposite of *ol'*. All things were of course originally *noo*, but you would never know it to look at the state of most of them now. *Noo* comes into its own when it characterises a loaf of bread recently taken from the oven, warm and soft on the inside, crusty and crackling on the outside and exuding a heavenly aroma that demands *ayt me*. It is strongly recommended that a purchaser makes haste to consume *noo* bread, as its quality is ephemeral and staleness is already getting ready to knock at tomorrow from beneath the crust. When the moon is coupled with *noo* it is said to be inadvisable to look at the lunar body through a glass window pane.

> *"What a laff twuz! Ol' Jessie oo zits down be th' front raw uv chairs under th' pulpit come t' church wearin' er noo shoes, en they wuz squaykin' like rats in a 'ay rick at drayshin time whenever er did move er vit!"*

In fond memory of Miss Jesie Pidler, aka Miss Pedlar, of Church Hill

Nuff

Nuff is neither too little nor too much. It is precisely the correct quantity that you require to satisfy your needs — which is not always a situation that Port Isaac boys are over-familiar with. Whoever it was that said *"Nuff be s' good 's a vaist"* would clearly not have been either a Port Isaac boy or one of his admiring sympathisers.

> *"Ev ee ad nuff?"*
> *"Whaddooee think mother?"*
> *"Ah dun't think nart! What ah do put on the taable never do be nuff fer ee!"*

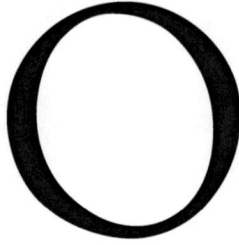

O

Oakey

A grove of trees all blessed with the height and thickness of trunk that speaks of great age and permanence, and which are made to appear more prominent by virtue of standing together in relative isolation. Although too restricted in terms of extent to be named as a wood, an *oakey* is somewhat more substantial than a mere copse.

> *"Th' rooks ev moved inta th' oakey up be th' top uv Freak valley! Ah zeed mebbe a score uv nests up there, en zome uv em dun't look t' be too ard t' git up to. Ef ee do be quick in yer climbin' ee kin git a rook's aig er doo aizy nuff. Mind ee, they birds maakes wan elluva racket when you'm comin, zo ef ee d' git caitched up a tree in th' oakey be ol' man Coppin frum th' varm, dun't ee tell un twuz me oo told ee bout th' aigs!"*

In fond memory of Mr Edgar "Old Egger" Bate of Church Hill

Ockin

For reasons that will already be clear to readers of this glossary, most Port Isaac people are not only certain to be unaware of the existence of a big word like **onomatopaeic** but also perfectly happy in being

144

unknowing. Did they but know it, *ockin* is a truly onomatopaeic word. *Ockin* incorporates all the elements of a procedure common to Port Isaac men, the harbinger of it being a noisy agitation at the back of the throat with the objective of elevating great gobs of *flem* up to the mouth, from whence they can then be expectorated with projectile-like velocity. If a spittoon is available to receive the discharge it is considered by the *ocker* to be something of a fine art to miss its aperture by the narrowest of margins.

> *"Me Uncle Sam do be a farty fag a day man en ev bin fer 'ears.*
> *A do be forever rattlin' a's chest en coffin en ockin up gobs s'big*
> *ez noo broke gull's aigs."*

Odds

In its purest sense, *odds* quantifies the mathematical probability that a gee-gee will lose you the two bob bet you placed "on its nose" with one of Port Isaac's two back-door bookies. However, since your credibility in picking winners is not exactly famed far and wide by your peers, let alone those bookies, to *odds ut* has come to define the hapless belief you have in your own expertise in this and other similarly critical trials of life.

> *"Th' vicar 'ad t' pick th' wan day in Awguss fer th' church*
> *fayte when th' rain come emptin' down!"*
> *"Aiz, you'm right. Ee cooden odds ut!"*

In fond memory of Mr Jack Hobbs of the New Coastguard Station

Ogg's puddin

A large and culturally diagnostic sausage, considered by the cognoscenti of Port Isaac to be a delicacy fit to liven the most jaded of palates. Any butcher worthy of the sawdust on his shop floor will be quick to declare that pork features in the recipe for his *ogg's puddin*, although as to the proportion of the sausage that is pork and exactly what the rest of the ingredients are is a mystery which the wise customer will make no attempt to solve. Deathly greyish-white in appearance in its natural state, the substance of an *ogg's puddin* is contained by a translucent skin, unpleasantly clammy to the touch, that is as unpleasant to contemplate as it is to consume in its raw state. Unlike revenge, *ogg's puddin* is a dish best not eaten cold; frying transversely cut slices of it is to be preferred.

> *"Ogg's pudding edden s' baad when ee ev's ut in a samwidge maade frum noo braid, jus' s' long ez ee do ev aichpee sauce t' ayve in un s'well. En dun't ee fergit t' taake off en git rids uv th' bleddy skins fust! Tez bes' though t' put the 'ogg's puddin' in th' ol' fryin' pan with a aig if ee kin git wan. A good bit uv lard en a ogg's pudding do fry up proper crisp en brown, en very taasty tez you!"*

In fond memory of Mr Wilfred Sandercock, master butcher of Middle Street

Ol'

Nominally, something or someone that is *ol'* is vested with age and is as often as not is observed to be a little the worse for wear. Although what is *ol'* is thereby construed as having nothing either *noo* or youthful about it, in its most celebrated use as a term of endearment, admiration or affection there is no limit to the age range over which it finds application.

> *"Arthur now, a's gittin' t' be a braave en ol' man oo wun't zee zeb'mty 'gaane. Ah likes un — a do be a good ol' bugger, en a's zon Jack do be a good ol' buhy too."*

Ollin

The art of making contumacious invective on the events of everyday life with your vocal delivery knob turned up to full volume. Anyone is at liberty to give *ollin* a go, but middle-aged Port Isaac ladies with a built-in sense of grievance against pretty much everything and everyone are its most adept exponents.

> *"Ef ee wuz t' go up t' th' council 'ouses, do ee maake shoo-er t' kaype clear uv number nahn en number zeb'm. They maids in they 'oussis lives jus' fer ollin' en shoutin' at aych other, though they'm appy t' oll en shout at any other poor bugger oo gits close nuff to em."*

Onsartin

You become *onsartin* when your state of mind is marked by a lack of self assurance. An *onsartin* person is an eternal pessimist when it comes to making predictions on the outcome of an event or activity that is just about to occur.

> *"Doo men come droo th' doo-er uv th' pub zinging that ol' zong bout ow 'Itler only ad wan ball! One uv em zayed twuz troo, but th' tother zayed a wuz a bit onsartin bout Goerin' evin' a cupla small wans, cuz Goerin' wuz sich a big fat bugger a should've ad a reel gurt pair uv bollicks on un."*

Oo

A word used to query someone's identity either by way of directly addressing him or by soliciting information from a third party who could be better informed about the said identity than you evidently are. Under the day-to-day pressures of life in Port Isaac it is not difficult to forget *oo* a chance acquaintance might be, and even more exacting to have to suffer the embarrassment of asking him for his name.

> *"Frum what th' vicar tol' we down be Zundy skool, Jaysus zayed, "Oo do be thy nayburr?" Well ah knaws oo me nayburr nex' doo-err do be, en ah do deerly wish ah dedden. Jaysus zayed s'well that us should love our nayburr, but ef a wants me t' love er, then the bugger ev got nother think comin."*

147

Oo-er

A rather long implement made of wood having a cross-section narrow enough to get your hand around so as to clasp it tight. An *oo-er* is smoothly rounded along most of its length and is trimmed flat at the leading end. It is used in a small sea-going craft in association with an articulate U-shaped metal device known as a *rollick* in a rhythmic action intended to induce the craft to make rapid way over the surface of the sea. A single *oo-er*, when set out and manipulated on a stern *rollick* to make a tight figure of eight action, imparts a forward motion referred to as *scullin*. Alternatively, a pair of *oo-ers* mounted in *rollicks* on either side of the central seat (the *thot*) of a boat are also able to create forward momentum when they are synchronised in a dipping action known as *rawin*. The word *rollick* is universally popular with Port Isaac County Primary School playground poets as a good rhyme for *bollick*. The great rafts of floating seaweed that often appear just offshore in the aftermath of a big Atlantic storm are called *oo-er wayd* for obvious reasons.

> *"What tez bout buhy, tez all a matter hov, that ee do knaw what you'm doin' uv. 'Arold now with wan oo-er kin scull a punt vaster en straighter than any doo other buggers rawin on th' middle thot with wan oo-er out on ayder zide!"*

In fond memory once again of Mr Frank "Nibs" Brown of upper Fore Street

Ope

A strait, tunnel-like passage established between two cottages in a terrace. An *ope* links a public thoroughfare with its ranks of mutely shut and paint-peeling front doors with a small enclosed courtyard flanked with ever-open back doors. Within the tight precincts of such courtyards the sun's rays penetrate only seldom and then at their peril. *Ope* passages of sufficient width and height to permit the entry of a horse-drawn cart are occasionally encountered, but tend

to be as scarce as was the alleged charity of those who once drove
horses through them.

> "*Granny Chabbang do be lucky er do ev a front doo-er onta*
> *th' strayte that er kin git inta er cottage droo, cuz zumwan s'*
> *big ez er do be cross the haass'd ev t' be shoved like a cark in a*
> *bottle in th' ole ope droo t' er back doo-er.*"

In fond memory of Gran Chadband of Dolphin Street

Orkard

Orkard describes the array of recognisable shortcomings in a
person's manner, deportment and sense of grace which combine to
make him or her (but chiefly him) appear clumsy and inarticulate.

> "*Ah never zeed no bugger lookin' s' orkard en cack 'anded ez ee*
> *do be. You'm like a cow 'andlin a musket!*"

Oss

An equine quadruped that, unlike a *gee-gee,* does not have wagers
placed on its ability to move more rapidly than others of its kind
between a starting gate and a winning post. The purpose of an *oss* is
set in hauling people and things from one place to another. Among
the typical duties of an *oss* are: the carriage of commercial freight;
dragging heavy items of farm machinery across waterlogged fields;
starring in universally popular cowboy films; and, as Mr Oscar
Wilde put it, assisting the unspeakable to go in full pursuit of the
uneatable.

> *King Cole went walkin down th' 'ill*
> *Be'ind a oss en cart.*
> *Whether twuz th' oss er he,*
> *Zumwan let a fart.*
> *The fart went rollin' down th' strayte—*
> *Ut knacked a p'leeceman off a's vit.*
> *Th' copper waaved a rusty pistol,*

Th' fart went 'ummin up t' Bristol.
Th' mayor uv Bristol wooden 'ome,
Th' fart went coosin' down t' Rome.
Th' Pope wuz aytin brayd en jam,
Th' fart run onwards t' Siam.
Ole King Kin wuz evin' a's din,
A opened a's mouth en th' fart rolled in.

A playground original

Tom Brown was a leading authority on western novels, and he once offered the following critique of the work of one of the genre's supreme authors, Mr Luke Short:

"That bugger's books be jus' s' good ez they be Clarincy Mulferd. When you'm raydin Luke Short you'm sartin t' be zittin on yer oss, gun in yer ann, en reddy fer th' fight comin up on t'other zide uv th' nex' river."

Out

(1) *Out* is the conventional response given by any Port Isaac boy when, on leaving home in the company of friends who have recently come calling for him, he is asked by his elders and betters to inform them *"juss where th' bleddy ell do ee think you'm guyne?"* The range of options covered by the concept of *out* is more or less infinite, and best left to the imagination.

> *"Jus where th' bleddy ell do ee think you'm guyne?"*
> *"Out."*
> *"Where to out?"*
> *"No plaace, jus' out!"*
> *"Thass awright then!"*

(2) The few bits and pieces of clothing that a true Port Isaac man actually owns are there to be worn, and worn to supreme

thinness of being is just what they get to be sooner or later—mostly sooner. Typically, wear of clothes takes place at the key points of contact abrasion such as the knees, the elbows, the backside, the toes and heels (for socks) and the toes and soles (of shoes). Once threadbare status has been reached disintegration quickly follows—patching and darning as a remedial measure are only able to hold back the tide in the short term. A condition described as being *more holey than righteous* then arrives and grades ever onwards into the celebrated sartorial situation known as being *out*.

> *"Whatever do ee look like? Yer boots could ev come frum a comic zinger they'm laffin' their toze off s' much, en ez fer yer cloze, they'm out t' haass en out t' helba. You'm a reel Dicky Doubt with yer shirt 'angin out!"*

Owbee-ee

A routine enquiry as to your current state of health as made by an acquaintance (or even a stranger) that you have met up with either by chance or design. Your response to *owbe-ee* will probably commence with one of the following aphorisms: (a) not bad; (b) not too bad; (c) can't complain; (d) couldn't be much worse even if it tried. Beyond these niceties, since the matter of health is far too important to be left to the compass of only a few words, reporting in detail on every ailment you have suffered for the past several years is mandatory, ending up more often than not with a bleak prognosis concerning your future prospects.

> *"Ullo there buhy, owbee-ee? Owzit guyne?"*
> *"Guyne? Ken't git much wuss buhy! Th' only plaace tez guyne with me do be down'ill purty fass, en thass jus' ow ee do be too ah s'pose."*

P

Paasty

It is a truth universally acknowledged that a Port Isaac man in possession of a good appetite must be in want of a *paasty*. Secure in a casing of pastry, the integrity of which is kept firm by a superficial rope-like pastry *crimp*; both of its *carners* replete with gravy; an interior stuffed with *mayte* (beef shin finely-cubed), *tetties*, *onyins* and perhaps some *turnup* for the more adventurous connoisseurs—earth hath not anything to show more fair. A *paasty* is also what a Port Isaac boy calls an individual segment of the orange that he immediately peels on finding it down at the foot of his pillow case in the very early morning of Christmas Day.

> *Fare vull, yer 'ansum paastry caase,*
> *Gurt Cap'n uv th' paasty raace!*
> *'Bove all croust do ee taake yer plaace,*
> *Best uv th' naation.*
> *Well be ee worthy uv God's graace,*
> *Blithe congregaashun!*
>
> *Me ayger 'andclasp ee do vill,*
> *Virm crimpin', twistin' like a rill,*

Swayte saavour risin' with a will
In luvvin' staym.
Yer carners tight with juices still,
No swayter draym!

Out with a knife ayged kayne with light,
T' cut ee up be mah delight.
Tetties and turnup, blendin' bright
In fraagrant 'ayte.
En then, caw what a gloorious zight!
Onyins en mayte!

Miner en visher be th' 'aid,
Rock, earth en zay rezave yer traid.
Blest 'eritidge uv blood ee shaid,
Vish, tin and copper.
Praaise be that they wuz paasty ved.
'Twus only proper!

Gurt powers that maakes mankind yer care,
En dishes up yer bill o' fare,
Port Isaac wants no dainty ware
Dressed up en naasty.
Zo ef ee wants our graateful prayer,
Give we a paasty!

Inspired by "To a Haggis" by the Bard of Ayr, Mr Robert Burns

Passel

A *passel* is a measure of a number of things or people assembled or gathered together in the same place at the same time. No specification of the actual quantity that makes a passel is necessary—as long as the number does not exceed how many digits you can see on your two hands (assuming you can count) any old estimate will be near enough. Port Isaac boys find, much to their regret, that the use of

153

passel as a collective noun for assholes probably didn't originate in the school playground, but for all that, they feel the lilt of this pair of words in combination rolls on their respective tongues in a mightily appealing way.

> *"There be th' vishermen, a gurt passel uv em, walkin' up en down, up en down fer aagies on the Town Platt, yarnin en spittin while they goes. Tez like time dun't mean nart t' they buggers, en ah tell ee buhy, time reely dun't."*

Passon

A clergyman ordained into the Church and given the title of vicar in order to serve the flock of churchgoers extant in the parish to which he is then assigned (St Endellion being a fine if not the finest example anywhere of such a parish) is a *passon*. As a reverend gentleman sermoniser, a *passon* ranks some way down in the hierarchy below the exalted *beshap* who resides down in Truro. Alternative sobriquets accorded to a *passon* in deference to his vocation are *praychur, bahbull puncher* and *'oly roller*—any of which can also be applied to a Chapel minister or a Chapel local preacher without fear of contradiction. The appellation *dog collar dick* however is unlikely to be applicable to a Chapel situation.

> *"Us do git all soorts up be Bood on th' noodiss baych. We ayben ev a passon oo comes 'long—ee kin zee un over there wearin uv a's dog collar so ever'body kin zee a do be a vicar."*
> *"Aiz, ah zeed un. Frum the look uv a's balls though, ah wooda thought a wuz a canon!"*

In fond memory of Port Isaac's greatest vicar ever, the Rev W. Atterbury Thomas

Patsta

A seafaring town located on the west side of the highly scenic estuary of North Cornwall's River Camel. A branch of the Southern Railway terminates at *Patsta* and there is a regular ferry service across the river between *Patsta* and the village of Rock, a godforsaken place inhabited almost exclusively by toffee-nosed members of the *Likes uv They*. A lifeboat of the RNLI, removed from Port Isaac (where it should truly belong) for reassignment, is now stationed in the *Patsta* harbour. Furthermore in the scheme of coastal administration, all commercial fishing boats that operate from ports within a radius of about ten miles of *Patsta* (which incorporates the Port Isaac fishing fleet) are registered to operate with an identity number provided with a *Patsta* (PW) prefix.

> "*The Zundy skool outin ez s'posed t' be guyne on a misstree trip, en zum do zay we'm off t' Patsta. Whatever be th' vicar thinkin uv? Ah wooden go t' Patsta ef they paid me fer ut. Patsta do ev nart t' zee en bugger all t'ayt en ef ee wuz t' tell me deffernt ah wooden b'leeve ee!*"

Pay Zoup

An ambrosial stew prepared from **lentulls, tetties, turnup, onyins** and a knuckle of ham. *Pay zoup's* peak of perfection is reached when the ham is so well cooked that it begins to fall away from the knuckle bone in tender shreds—just as well that it does perhaps, since a knuckle consists of much bone and little meat. The crowning glory of *pay zoup* comes when it is served in association with slices of currant-studded *figgy duff*. *Pay zoup* is not a dainty dish, but a queen could do a lot worse than have it set before her.

> "*Zorry ah ken't stop, Ah got t' 'urry t' git t' Gran's fer dinner time. Er's maakin' pay zoup en ef ah comes laate th' only bits uv the knuckle lef' fer me'll be fat, skin en bone.*"

In loving memory of Mrs Eleanor "Gran" Creighton of Canadian Terrace

Peckchurs

The *peckchurs* are, as far as a Port Isaac boy is concerned, the paramount form of public entertainment. *Peckchurs* are characterised by moving images projected from special photographic film onto a tautly spread vertical white sheet (technically known as a *skrayn*) that once a week for every week of the good old year boosts the spirits of the many regular cinemaphiles whose backsides grace the indifferent seating arrangements of which the Port Isaac Rivoli cinema (a converted garage) is justifiably proud. A typical evening's entertainment at the *peckchurs* consists of a *big peckchur* preceded by either a *little peckcher* or a so called *vull zuppoortin programme*. The boys who occupy the rows of wooden benches up at the front of the Rivoli favour *big peckchurs* dealing with the active deeds of, among others: cowboys and indians; cops and robbers; Tarzan; and Abbot and Costello. At a pinch the boys are prepared to tolerate *moosick peckchurs* starring Fred Astaire and Ginger Rogers, but they have a dedicated antipathy to *kissin peckchurs* and make their views on the latter evident through stamping their feet and groaning repeatedly to relieve the tedium until such time as they are evicted by the Rivoli's honorary usher Mr Roseveare.

> *"Afower th' big peckchur comes on us gits t' zee things like "Chraahme Dun't Pay" en "Pete Smith Speshaltees" en "Passin' Paarade", en "Pathy Noos" what only do be a foo months ol'. What us deerly likes bess though be "Popeye the Zailor"! Popeye do ayt spinach en us dun't, but us kin zing a's zong fer un when a starts—*
>
> *Ah be Popeye th' zailor man,*
> *Ah lives in a caravan.*
> *Th' girls do be dirty,*
> *They lifts up me shirty,*
> *En tickles me marzipan!*

In fond memory of Mr Charlie Lobb and Mr Roseveare, both of Back Hill

Pelchurd

A relatively small fish of gigantic commercial value, the physical appearance of a *pelchurd* is remarkably similar to that of a herring. *Pelchurds* move through the briny deep in vast shoals presenting highly desirable targets for the attention of fishermen. As far as is known, the fate of the multitudes of *pelchurds* caught is to be gutted, cleaned, cooked and packed into flat tins where they are tightly sealed in the company of what is either euphemistically described as oil, or alternatively a medium which has a passing reference to tomato sauce. The inspiration for tinning *pelcherds* is believed to have come from consideration of the Black Hole of Calcutta. The expression *crame on pelchurds* denotes excellence, and forms an enduring tribute to the role this important fish has played in developing the North Cornish fishing industry.

> *"One time, Port wuz th' voo-erth biggist vishin' port en all uv Carnwall fer landin' caitches uv pelchurds. T'day there edden s'much es wan pelchurd comin into all uv th' bleddy Bay, en ef ee do want t' zee zeverl pelchurds t'gether 'gain tez naydid t' open wan uv they tins up."*

Pisky

In Cornish folk lore (in respect of which it may be said to call the tales legion, for they are many), a *pisky* is a highly retiring humanoid creature of diminutive stature. Traditionally a *pisky* is believed to wear a tall pointed hat while reclining on top of a toadstool in order to conduct its deliberations—it is not clear if such free spirits are male or female by gender or whether or not they operate independently or in groups. It is, however, alleged that the *modus operandi* of a *pisky* is the bringing of good luck to anyone who truly believes in its existence, even if no-one who has ever seen a *pisky* is known to have lived to tell the tale.

"A pisky kin bring ee luck jus' s'long as ee dun't zee un. They do zay that only they oo ben't long fer this world zees un atall. Ee would ev t' belong in Bommin t' g'wout lookin fer un. Mine ee though, a pisky dun't go round 'idin pots uv gold be th' end uv rainbows like they leprycorns fer we t' vind. Us ben't that lucky in Port!"

Platt

An open flat(tish) area of common ground located more or less centrally in a town or village, a *platt* serves the general public as a place where social gatherings both large and small, formal and informal can be conducted. It thereby performs a similar function to that of a village green, although it has to be admitted that the only greenery associated with the Port Isaac Town Platt is to be found in an occasional lonely weed rooted in the dust of ages in an overlooked corner.

"There always do be a braave en gurt congreegaashin fer th' fust 'im down be th' open air sarvice they evs Zundy aybenins on th' Town Platt when th' aybenins is gittin drawed out. But ef th' praychur do go on fer too long, then with openin' time up be the pub come seb'ma clock, the congreegaashin do thin out vast doorin th' zarmin."

Port

Port is the One and Only. It is the given name of the finest village on the coast of North Cornwall—or for that matter anywhere else on the Cornish coastline—not to mention any other coastline anywhere else in the world. *Port's* full title is Port Isaac, but just plain *Port* does very nicely to define its uniqueness to those who call it home thank you very much.

Port men ev gone off en zailed th' zays, all zeb'm,
En zome uv em ev come back ome agaane, en zum uv em ebben.

158

Whatever they d' do ah laive ee thicky wan pure thought t' enjuhy.

Ee kin taake th' buhy out uv Port, but ee ken't taake Port out uv th' buhy.

Proper

As applied to a person, a thing or a deed, *proper* implies a supreme level of quality that is both optimal and constructive in every respect. An *emmet's* criticism of something believed to be *proper* will be taken up as a deadly insult to be avenged by any *proper* Cornishman.

"Ev ee done yer skool 'omework?"
"Jus' vineeshed un."
"Thass a proper job!"

Purty

Since *purty* bears some relationship of meaning to *proper,* for which it can be taken to represent a poor man's synonym for the latter, it is not considered to be a bad accolade when it is awarded.

"Zince they put th' noo manager over be th' bleddy Kwop the plaace do be run purty 'gain."

In fond memory of Mr William Auger of lower Trewetha Lane

Pusser's brekfiss

A no-frills repast at the commencement of the daily grind, it would be nice if a *pusser's brekfiss* could set the tone in which you would like the day to continue, as distinct from the depressing way in which the day will most probably drag on. The items on the menu for a *pusser's brekfiss* are two in number, namely a smoke and a shit.

"Will ee look et Vera, mutton dressed like mutton, en a faace on 'er that maakes ee think uv a pusser's brekfiss."

With thanks to Mr Donald "Kenty" Kent of Hartland Road

Q

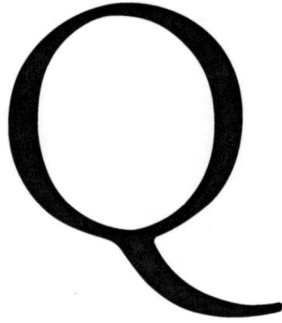

Port Isaac people keep a weather eye open for any word commencing with the letter Q in order that they may instantly eschew its use in conversation.

"Words that begins with koos, they ben't fer th' Likes uv We."

R

Raaslin

A gaily competitive Cornish contact sport involving two half-naked muscular men grappling at one another's slippery bodies within a circle of restricted space. These shoulder-to-shoulder contestants (referred to as *raaslers*) shuffle about in a crab-like manifestation of bent backs and locked arms, each endeavouring to gain an advantage of balance that can allow him to tumble the other to the ground in order to be declared the victor. As enervating as *rasslin* may be for its participants, spectators with a low boredom quotient soon tend to find themselves short of much to get excited about.

> *"In John Glover, Port ev got a bonny feed Carnish rasslin champeen. John kin thraw more'n two times a's awn weight, en there eb'm bin a vahner pair uv shoulders zeed on any bugger zince Strang th' Terubble put on a's lepperd skin in th' Adventure."*

In fond memory of Mr John Glover of Middle Street

Rabbut

A long-eared, bob-tailed creature of the wild which lives and thrives in enormous underground communities called **warrins** that connect up to the surface via an intricate set of tunnels referred to as **burras**. **Rabbuts** are prolific throughout the fields, woodlands, valley bottoms and cliff-fringed redoubts of St Endellion parish. Although preyed on constantly by buzzards, owls, foxes, farmers, dogs, cats, all casual holders of shotguns and/or air rifles and setters of snares and gins, the breeding habits of **rabbuts** are so intensive that the overall population tends to remain steady as she goes. That a **rabbut** forms the principal ingredient for the perennially popular **rabbut** pie is a glorious thing for Port Isaac boys to ponder on, God be praised!

> *"Afore ee gits roun' t' skinnin thacky rabbut ee've bin en shot s'marnin, kin ee kaype wan uv a's vit fer me playze? They do zay a rabbut's voot'll bring ee luck, en ah kin do with zome uv thack."*
>
> *"Aiz, ah shall kaype a voot fer ee, but ah ev t' tell ee, the voot dedden bring bugger all in th' way uv luck t' th' bleddy rabbut!"*

And, with many thanks to Mr Ted Robinson, Port Isaac raconteur extraordinaire, here are some lines adapted from a Temperance Hall pantomime lyric which that great man, inspired by the popular song "Ma, She's Making Eyes At Me", penned for the delectation of the general public of his post-war day:

> *Ma, 'er's baakin' pies fer me!*
> *Mayte (aiz mayte) en rabbut pies fer me!*
> *Ma, er've jus' 'bout broke both me teeth*
> *With 'er baakin',*
> *My gar, 'ow me belly's aakin!*
> *Ma, 'er wants t' murder me*
> *With 'er tall paas-try!*
> *Now 'er've maade the crust much thicker,*
> *When ah gits 'ome ah'm guyne kick 'er!*
> *Ma, er's killin' me!*

Rag

The process by which a neat construction of a relatively flimsy nature is converted into a *Lanson Jail*-like rearrangement of its constituents through either a deliberate act of vandalism or simply for the pure fun of the moment. A bird's nest can be inadvertently *ragged* from the cumulative attention of far too many boys' hands exploring it for the presence of seasonal eggs.

> *"Tez time fer ee t' go down t' the barber me ansum. Yer air do look as ef t'ev bin ragged be a gang uv gypsies."*
>
> In fond memory of Mr Barry Anderson of lower Front Hill

Raydinenrytin

The two subjects which bear such an intimate relationship the one to the other that they are always linked in thought, and which are drummed with mixed success into the boys and girls of Port Isaac down at the County Primary School, are spoken of in combination as *raydinenrytin*. The *raydin* part of the couplet involves the visual interpretation of words in print, whereas the *rytin* supplement demands orderly manual transfer of the spoken word to paper through the medium of pen and ink. The first problem which most of those that are taught *raidinenrytin* have to face up to is to work out which of the two subjects is which. *Raydin* is always easier when the words have got lots of pictures connected with them.

> *"What woodee like t' ev fer yer birfdy? Ee idden too baad be raydinenrytin—kin Granfer en me git a book fer ee?"*
> *"Naw thanks Gran, ah awreddy got wan."*

Raw

Raw defines the nature of milk drawn only recently from a cow once it gets transferred directly into your enamel basin at home from the milkman's delivery bucket by means of a dipper. *Raw* milk is left to stand in the said basin for a few hours prior to the basin being placed over a source of slow heat to induce the milk to scald and the cream to separate, cool and clot in time for tea.

> *"We ev's doo pintsa milk aych marnin frum Mr 'Illson out uv a's buckit. Our plaace be th' fust on a's milk round down frum th' varm, zo when we gits ut th' milk be raw en staymin as tez dipped inta th' baasin fer we."*

With further reference to *raw* it should be read, marked, learned and inwardly digested that it is also specifies a great delicacy found inside a herring as well as the two-oars-in-combination technique of pulling a punt around the harbour. A line of *teeled tetties* is a *raw* as well. Hence context is all as far as interpretation of the word is concerned.

Reely

To understand the meaning of *reely* you can do no better than refer to the ever-smiling Uncle Remus in Walt Disney's film *Song of the South*—"It's the truth, its actual, everything is satisfactual!" The fundamental characteristic of *reely* is that only *reel* Cornish people can pronounce it in a *proper* way. No matter how thoroughly the Cornish are taught elocution, no matter how severely their native accent gets to be starched and smoothed under the iron fist of time and the steady depredations of the *Likes uv They*, when a Cornishman opens his mouth and pronounces the word *reely* he is endorsed, stamped, sealed and seen for what he is, and his *jacker* roots are exposed in all their glory.

> *"Whabbee guyne do when ee layves skool?"*
> *"Ah reely dun't knaw ait, but ah do be shoo-er ah ben't guyne be nayder a taychur ner a praychur, cuz ah've reely ad nuffa they buggers awreddy t' las' me ferever."*

164

Rish

When you are impelled to move with urgent despatch as needs must, time having finally ceased to be on your side, you are said to be in a *rish*. However the act of *rishin round* is so alien to a Port Isaac way of life that whenever it is seen happening to someone it is regarded as a true phenomenon.

> *"Frank down be Middle Strayte do gener'ly move round slawer'n a tortiss. Ah only ever zeed un rish anywhere on a cupple occaashuns, wance when a wuz right on th' pint uv bein' laate fer openin' time, en wance when a wuz took a bit shoo-ert on the way op t' th' Post Office t' zend a's pools off. Ayben zo, ah ben't too shoo-er that th' ol' bugger wooden zooner shit a'zelf'n ev t' rish."*

Rubbeesh

Material generated in the cottage environment that is no longer wanted on the grounds of it being either inedible, useless, obsolete, defunct or irretrievably broken is considered to represent *rubbeesh*. Among procedures used for the disposal of *rubbeesh* are formal delivery to the council dust cart, a clandestine drop into one of the abandoned mineshafts up in the valley, and a traditional classic *ayve* over the cliff.

> *Mah ol' man do be a dustman—*
> *Et the battle uv Waterloo,*
> *A cleared up all th' rubbeesh,*
> *When a wuz ayty-doo.*
> *Zome lay ere,*
> *Zome lay there,*
> *Zome lay roun' th' carner.*
> *Wan poor zole*
> *With a bullet up a's 'ole*

Come runnin roun' th' carner
Zingin, "Water, water!"
Water come et las',
Ah dun't want yer water
Ee kin stick et up yer . . .
Haass no questions
Tell no lies,
Ah zeed a copper
A doin up a's . . .
Flies be a noosince
Bugs be wuss,
Whaddoo ee think
Uv mah little verse?"

A playground original

Runner-in

Someone who hails from foreign parts (which by definition means anywhere outside the virtual walls that generations of inbreeding have thrown up all along the boundary of St Endellion parish) and who comes to dwell among the **Likes uv We** is classified as a **runner-in**. This designation is invested with no positive attributes. Far too many **runners-in** exhibit the kind of airs and graces that Port Isaac people find abhorrent in everyone apart from themselves. No time limit is set on the longevity of a **runner-in** stamp. The stigma of it is such that, once attached, it very possibly may never be removed.

> *"Th' Arbour Caffy ev bin awned be ol' Ted ever zince a comed down t' live ere bout dirty 'ear back with a's fambly. We likes all uv em, but mind ee, none uv 'em edden nart but runners in."*

S

Sartin

The opposite of *onsartin*. Oft-cited type-examples of things that are *sartin* are death, taxes, the fact that there are far too many *miser'ble ol' buggers* living in Port Isaac, and the knowledge that the *bleddy council* in Wadebridge will never act in the best interests of its ratepayers, no matter how many flowery promises the councillors might like to make to the contrary.

> *"Ah do be a straanger t' Port Isaac—kin ee tell me 'ow ah kin git down t' th' Town Platt playze?"*
>
> *"Well now missis, tez fer ee t' git down th' ol' 'ill a piece, then ee do ev t' taake a right turn, er mebbe tez a left turn, ah kin nivver zay which uv em do be which."*
>
> *"Ee edden very sartin buhy, be ee?"*
>
> *"Ah do be sartin ah ben't lookin' fer th' Town Platt like ee be doin', en thass sartin nuff fer me!"*

Scritchin

A highly emotive condition typically featuring voluntarily inspired lachrymation accompanied by open-mouthed wailing. *Scritchin* may either arise in response to an external stimulus or be contrived in keeping with the pursuit of ulterior motives. The most adept practitioners of *scritchin* are often referred to as *skwaalhaasses*.

> *"That maid oo do live down th' road frum we do be a reel skwaalhaass. Ah calls she Vi'let Lizibit—er kin git on scritchin en scritchin til' er do be zick, jus' cuz er kin."*

Scrumpin

A seasonal pleasure involving boys relieving privately owned apple trees of as much of their burden of fruit as the immediate infrastructure permits. The boys endeavour (not always successfully) to make their moves when the owner of the apple trees is believed to be absent from the general locality. *Scrumpin* may be regarded as technical *theevin*, but Port Isaac boys don't worry too much about *theevin* as long as the spoils are edible. Although in principle *scrumpin* can be directed at gardens replete with strawberries, raspberries, blackcurrants and even young white turnips, its prime target is orchard-based fruit. Lifting and pocketing apples from display arrangements in the church at harvest festival time is considered to be not altogether out of tune with the noble spirit of *scrumpin*.

> *"Wance me aapples do start t' git rahpe, ah do ev t' waitch th' ol' archard like a bleddy 'awk. The buhys comes reg'lar, scrumpin off all they kin git their theevin ans on. Ah'll give they buggers scrumpin ef ah ever gits 'old uv they!"*

In memory of a certain orchard up in the Port Quin valley

Scud

A *scud* is an attractive crust, normally russet-brown in colour, that develops slowly but surely on your skin in the aftermath of a decent cut, scratch or graze. The best kinds of *scuds* are found on knees and/or elbows that have been skinned in consequence of a sudden and unexpected impact with a hard and abrasive surface. During their formational stages, *scuds* beg to be picked at with the fingers, yet the longer the temptation to pick at them can be resisted the more satisfying the final product is likely to be. Ideally a *scud* should be left *in situ* to mature until it can be peeled away to expose fresh, pink, well-healed skin beneath — and then, with its job done, it can be placed on the tongue to be consumed with gratification.

> *"Neerly all they buhys oo plays vootball in th' skool playground do ev scuds all over their naze. Zome uv 'em ev got scuds on top uv scuds. They plays 'ard ah kin tell ee."*

Shank

A well-proportioned black-feathered bird of the coast, cliffs and seascape along Port Isaac Bay, a *shank* is a close and slightly smaller relative of the cormorant. It bears a modest tuft-like crest on its head. *Shanks* like to congregate in substantial numbers on wave-washed rocks and promontories — their stock in trade is diving underwater to catch fish. When seen swimming in the sea, close enough inshore to be within earshot, a *shank* can be induced to dive when instructed to do so by an observer, who then has the excitement of betting his friends precisely where he thinks the *shank* will be likely to resurface. The formal guidebook name for this fine figure of a bird is a **shag**, but their elders and betters, for reasons unexplained to Port Isaac boys, have outlawed the use of that name, and have instead come down in favour of referring to the bird as *shank*.

> *Shanky shanky doodle,*
> *Vish under water!*
> *Shanky,*
> *Shanky doodle,*
> *Vish under water!*

The chant of a Port Isaac schoolboy when he observes a *shank* in the harbour

She

The third person feminine singular pronoun, *she* is the distaff side of *a* and is synonymous, more or less, with *er*. An average Port Isaac character is inclined, in one of life's little ironies, to use *she* where *er* might have been preferable, and naturally enough vice versa. A satisfactory explanation for this curious state of juxtaposition has yet to be discovered.

> "*Where be er to these days?*"
> "*Ah ebben zeed she fer zeverl waykes, but ah did 'ear that er run off t' Plymuff with a trav'lin man.*"
> "*Oo wuz a?*"
> "*Dun't knaw maid, though ooever a wuz, jus' s'long ez a wuz wearin' trowsis t'wooden matter much t' the Likes uv She.*"

Shet

The action of lowering a line of baited crab pots—linked one to the other with lengths of good tarred rope and terminating with a marker buoy—from the deck of a fishing boat to the sea bed where it will hopefully attract the attention of crabs and lobsters.

> "*Us shet near on hunderd pots a wayke back, and when us pulled em s'marnin all us got wuz doo spider crabs en vahve bleddy star vishes! Ayben Jaysus cooden veed th' vahve thousin' with they!*"

In appreciation of the Port Isaac fishing fleet

Shit

No surprises here! *Shit* as a substance is exactly what you surmise it to be. Various among the *Likes uv They* and their ilk are known to believe that their personally generated brand of this ubiquitous commodity doesn't stink, but who are they kidding? Allowing for the fact that he omitted the fabled *"number two"*, Tony "Bollicks" Robinson's classic playground mantra *"dung shit jobby shite poop crap"* effectively covers a good range of alternative terms for this popular word.

> *In days uv old,*
> *When knights wuz bold,*
> *En lavatrees wooden inventid.*
> *They digged a pit,*
> *En 'ad a shit,*
> *En went 'way contentid.*
>
> *In days uv old,*
> *When knights wuz bold,*
> *En paaper wooden inventid.*
> *The pulled zome grass,*
> *En wiped their haass,*
> *En went 'way contented.*

Another playground original

And in addition:

> *"Whaddoo ee think uv that noo 'otel up be th' Terrice?"*
> *"Tez S-H-I-T buhy!"*
> *"Mah gar, do ee mayne tez th' Smartist Hotel In Town?"*
> *"Buhy, when ah do spell shit, ah maynes shit!"*

While not forgetting:

> *"Why dedden ee cloze th' bleddy doo-er when ee wuz guyne out?"*
> *"Ah thought ah did cloze un!"*
> *"Ee knaws what thought did, dun't ee?"*

171

"What did a do?"
"A thought a'd shit azelf, en a 'ad!"

Skee-daddle

When you *skee-daddle* you are undertaking a rapid exit from the scene of a developing situation just as if you were being pursued by Shakespeare's bear, thereby demonstrating a firm belief in discretion being the better part of valour.

> *"Whether er not us ev jus' did zumthin good er bad, when us zees th' pleeceman comin' long th' strayte, tez time fer we t' skee-daddle. That pleeceman kin clayre a strayte when a shaws up in zackly th' zaame way that a dose uv caster ile do coose th' shit out uv ee."*

Skerrick

A tiny portion of a whole, not much more perhaps than a shred or a fragment of an entity. In principle a *skerrick* could specify a fallen crumb from a rich man's table granted to a Port Isaac supplicant. Coming closer to home however, a *skerrick* is most definitely what a boy expects to be left with when others, notably his elders and betters, have as usual grabbed more than their fair share at dinner time.

> *"Be th' time ah come in laate fer me dinner, all that wuz left uv th' rice puddin' wuz th' dish. There wooden ayben a skerrick uv skin t' be 'ad after some bugger oo shall be naameliss did scraape th' zides uv th' dish down t' th' 'nammel with a's spoon."*

Skittery

A serendipitous quality ascribed to any inclined surface gifted with such a minimal coefficient of friction that an object placed on it encounters little or no resistance to gliding or sliding down the *skittery* slope.

> *Up be th' mountin'*
> *Skittery graass,*
> *A man falled down*
> *En skitter'd on a's haass.*
> *Th' man shit a monkey,*
> *Th' monkey shit a flay,*
> *Th' flay shit a staymeboat,*
> *En they all went out t' zay.*

Lines believed to have been composed by an idle group of boys at Lobber Point

Skivver

A piece of wood approximately a foot long that has been whittled down to approximately half an inch in diameter prior to being modestly notched at the half way point and shaved to needle sharpness on one extremity. A *skivver* thus complete is used to impale and secure bait, in the typical form of an exceedingly over-ripe gurnard, to the inside bottom of a withy-woven crab pot. Once the pot has been properly *shet*, the noisome presence of the bait will, with a bit of luck, entice hungry crabs and/or lobsters to make their way into the pot via its entry port of no return.

> "*T'wood be interstin t' knaw ef skivvers could be maade be a masheen. Still, s'far as ut do go, tez pretty sartin that a visherman with a bit uv wood en a sharp knife'd alwys maake a proper wan. Ol' Nibs kin trim ee a skivver with a pint on un fit fer t' darn a zock with.*"

In memory of winter evenings at Fishermen's Classes in the Slipway House garage

173

Skool

An institution that in the perception of a Port Isaac boy is run for no other reason than for the self-gratification of a band of ruthless martinets named *taychurs* who are bound to perform their savage duties under the dictates of an autocrat bearing the title of *aidmaaster*. A typical *skool* like Port Isaac County Primary provides education enforced by chastisement for the boys and girls of the village and its outlying satellite communities. These children, formally referred to as *poopulls*, are obliged by both law and avoidance of the wrath of their parents to be at the *skool* for a pre-ordained number of hours every day from Monday through Friday of each week. Come wind, come weather, to *skool* they have to go, whether the *skool* be *prymerry* (as in Port Isaac), *secundree* (over in Wadebridge) or *grammer* (up to Camelford). The *taychurs* weather rough seas as they battle to instil in their uncomprehending charges the rudiments of a number of *subjicks*, among which are to be found:

Raydin	Words to look at in books
Rytin	Words to put down on paper with a pen and ink
Riffmettick	Adding up, taking away, multiplying and dividing numbers
Joggerfy	Other places in the world
Istree	What was supposed to have happened a long time ago
Drawin	Making pictures
Aljebber	*Riffmettick* using letters in place of numbers
Jommatree	Shapes and Angles
Kemusstree	Mixing chemicals to make smells
Fizzicks	Electricity, pressure and stuff like that
Ingleesh Langwidge	How to talk proper and use *grammer*
Ingleesh Littertoor	Books and poems written donkeys' years ago

| *Lattin* | A language nobody speaks any more, apart from *Cafflick* priests who don't count |

"Th' miser'ble bugger oo zaid that skool days wuz the 'appiest days uv a's life, never wuz in Enery Pam's class be Port skool! Ef a wuz, a wood've knawed better."

Skoo-wiff

Whatever "kilter" is assumed to mean when it is applied to an assessment of the quality of something or other, anything that is reckoned to look *skoo-wiff* is very much the opposite of that definition. Forget rectilinearity and orderly assembly, *skoo-wiff* defines an-out-of shape condition with all the elements of *Lanson Jail* thrown in for good measure. The sort of *haassboutfaace* thing that is *skoo-wiff* is common enough in everyday life in Port Isaac for it to go unremarked as a rule.

"A do be s' cack-anded that ayben ef a knawed 'ow to use a ruler t' maake a margin in a's rytin book t'wood still come out all skoo-wiff."

Skullard

The antithesis of a *dullard*, a *skullard* is someone who, having by general consensus received too much *bleddy* education for his own good, nevertheless appears to have won at least a few admirers from among the ranks of his *taychurs*. Naturally well-read, he is able to converse with ease on a wide range of topics and in doing so to demonstrate sufficient breadth of general knowledge to earn him plaudits. Synonyms for *skullard* are *longaided*, *eddycaatid* and *braaney*. With that said, there is some truth in the rumour that bullshit artists and *skullards* share a common bond.

"Do ee knaw 'ow var tez t' git frum 'ere t' Lundin?"
"Dun't ee ast me buhy! Owevver var tez, tez too var fer me t'

think 'bout. T'wood be bes' ef ee wuz t' go en ask uv th' vicar
when ee zees un nex'. That bugger do be a reel skullard, en
ayben ef a dun't knaw th' anser, a'll tell ee zumthin' t' maake
ee think a do."

Slaypin

A state of dormancy unifying both mind and body which is a
perennial favourite with Port Isaac people. *Slaypin* soothes away
the trials and tribulations of life with the gift of repose in the arms
of Morpheus (or anyone else as far as that goes) for as much as
a number of durable hours to as little as a few fleeting moments.
Although *slaypin* usually finds its ideal place during the hours
of darkness, no time of day can ever be said to be not eminently
suitable for its practice.

> *Now Draake, a's in a's 'ammick,*
> *Till th' gurt Armarders come.*
> *Cap'n, be ee slaypin there below?*

With thanks to Sir Henry Newbolt

Slock

A mystic art (believed by the cognoscenti to verge on black magic of
the non-chocolate kind) permitting those who are gifted with it to
successfully entice a feline to transfer its allegiance from one home
to another without coercion.

> *"When Thelma dedden come t' skool twuz zayed that th'*
> *gypsies 'ad took 'er, but twuz no such luck fer we reely, cuz 'er*
> *wuz only in bayd with th' oopin coff. Tez troo that the gypsies*
> *wants that maid though, cuz er kin slock cats aizy, en 'er do*
> *be a proper wan fer zettin' curses ez us all do knaw only too*
> *well."*

In fond memory of Miss Thelma Bennett of the Poor Court

Slone

The fruit of the mayblossom tree, a ripe *slone* looks like a very small plum, deep blue-black in colour with a delightfully irridescent bloom on its skin. Comparison with a plum goes no further than this however, as a *slone* offers little flesh around its stone. Such flesh as there is has a sourly astringent taste that few can tolerate. Prolific quantities of *slones* are picked in the autumn by many boys and girls to be taken home and used to make batches of domestic *slone* wine and *slone* gin—subsequently imbibed purely for medicinal purposes of course.

> *"Afower they gits too big, grayn slones be good fer firin frum a payshooter er a cattypalt. When the slones gits blue we always trys t'ayt uv em, but all they'm good fer then do be maakin yer mouth dry out."*

Slops

The breakfast of necessity for Port Isaac boys when all entreaties for fried bread with a spread of treacle have failed and the porridge packet is once again discovered to be empty. *Slops* are prepared using the following tried and true recipe—cut a couple of slices from a loaf of bread that has been around long enough to be new no longer; trim the slices (including the crust) into small squares and place the same in a basin; sprinkle as much sugar on top of the bread as you can get away with before someone stops you; pour hot milk over it all; and eat it up before the milk can get cold. Other names for this non-Lucullan delight are *milky sue* and *braidenmelk*, although neither of these sums up the slimy texture and make-do character of the concoction as well as *slops* does.

> *"Gimmee a gurt baasin uv slops, a cup o' tay en a fag fer brekfiss, en ah do be zet till dinner time."*

177

Splitter

A soft white bread roll—one of an always even number of rolls baked together in close enough proximity to form a combined batch. You separate an individual *splitter* from the batch merely by inserting your thumbs on the side joins then dragging the thumbs sideways. A *splitter* is best eaten when it is new. Pulled (or split) open across the middle, each consequent half makes a base for a spread of jam topped by a big gob of clotted cream. *Emmets* need to note that the cream goes on top of the jam and not vice versa.

> *"Will ee playze coose down t' th' baakers en git us zecks noo splitters fer our tay? Maake shoo-er ee do git em in a baitch en not broke up, so that they stays noo en dun't dry out afore we ayts em."*

In fond memory of Sherratt's bakery in lower Fore Street

Stenkin

The diagnostic characteristic of an aroma which creates, to say the least, an unwelcome assault on the olfactory glands of all who stray within range of its pungency. Odour of the body kind is not reckoned to be proper *stenkin*, since no matter how rank it may be, Port Isaac people all possess body odour to a greater or lesser degree and would miss it if it wasn't there.

> *Aw deer, what kin th' matter be?*
> *Dree ol' laadies locked in th' lavatree.*
> *Bin there ever zince Zatdy.*
> *Nobody knawed they wuz there!*
>
> *Mah gar, zo much skulduggery!*
> *Door locked be zome kind uv thuggery.*
> *Inzide, stenkin like buggery.*
> *Nobody knawed they wuz there!*

In fond memory of the Misses Jessie Pidler, Fanny Fuzz Bush, and Alice Brown

Stick

A term describing small pieces of firewood which have been repeatedly split away from large logs along the grain by cutting, chopping, hacking or applying any other form of severance rooted in brute force and ignorance. *Stick* is used to both start and sustain the miracle of fire in the cottage hearth. It is essential that the wood from which *stick* is prepared should not only be non-green but also dry. Ideal *stick* can be derived from pieces of **wreck**, deadfallen trees and boughs from up in the woods, and commercially obtained sawn logs—but please be warned, the latter tend to promote deposits of soot in the chimney after long-term use. In an emergency, council-house skirting boards and banisters will also make excellent *stick*.

> "*Ef you'm guyne up th' bottoms will ee taake a zack 'long with ee, then on yer way 'ome ee kin c'leck a bit uv stick fer th' vire.*"

T

Tacker

This word has such an obvious maritime association that a seafaring man (or even a Port Isaac fisherman) almost certainly placed horny hands on its etymology. A *tacker* is a highly active (some would say over-active) boy of tender years and diminutive proportions. He is little in essence—there is no such thing as a **gurt tacker**. Elderly men down on the Town Platt like to recall constantly, with reference to today, just how much better life in general was when they were *little tackers*. Age has, however, turned some of them into such miserable old buggers that it has to be suspected they were born with old heads on *tacker* shoulders.

> *"Ah dedden go'way t' vight no bleddy war zo ah could come 'ome in me dee-mob suit en ev little tackers givin' me a mouffull uv cheek on the strayte. En mah day little tackers wuz zeed en not 'eard, en thass what us wuz vightin 'Itler t' old onta!"*

With many thanks to Mr E. W. (Bill) Platt

Tay

Call *tay* what you will—the nectar of the gods; the cup that cheers but does not (worse luck!) inebriate; the poor man's solace; or perhaps the stuff that dreams are made of—there is no doubt that life in Port Isaac would present itself as more of a burden than it already is if, in the cottage cupboard, a half-pound packet of the unassumingly dark and dry wisps of *tay*, that in their green prime graced lush hills in India and Ceylon was absent. The rules for making a *proper dish uv tay* are no more than two in number: (1) enough *tay* must be spooned from *taypacket* to *taypot* (not forgetting the vital extra *tayspoonvull* for the pot) to ensure a brew figuratively strong enough to stand the *tayspoon* up in when boiling water is added to infuse; and (2) milk (not too much) must be poured into the *dish* in advance of the *tay*, and not (repeat not) vice versa. Once the maximum colour of the infusion has been liberated and all the *tay* has been imbibed down to the very last drop, what is left in the *taypot* to be discarded is *taylayves*—popular places for their disposal are down the outside lavatory bowl and in the kitchen sink. The *taylayves* which are seen at the bottom of a *dish* are understood to have taken on a pattern decreed by fate, and for good or ill when their distribution is analysed by an expert, the prospects for the immediate future of he or she who drank the *tay* in the *dish* will be made crystal clear.

> *Wan, doo, dree,*
> *Mother catched a flay,*
> *Er put un in th' taypot*
> *T' maake a dish uv tay.*
> *Th' flay jumped out,*
> *Mother gived a shout,*
> *Down come faather*
> *With a's shirt angin' out.*

Another playground original

181

Teelin

Teelin embodies the entire gamut of dedicated attention that an industrious gardener lavishes on the soil of his garden or allotment in order to ready the plot for the annual sowing of seeds, plants and tubers—that roll of honour comprising cabbage, broccoli, cut-and-come-again, sprouts, *bacca*, onion sets, shallots, *tetties*, runners, broad beans and so on. Well, you get the drift. The fertility of the garden soil is greatly enhanced by the addition during *teelin* of generous quantities of either one or both of seaweed and animal shit (cow, horse and sheep varieties being preferred).

> *In a kwaary,*
> *Teelin tetties,*
> *Be a man uv bone and skin.*
> *En a's naame ez*
> *Jimmy Baaker,*
> *En a's prick be like a pin.*

With many thanks to Messrs Leonard (Buh) Honey and Jimmy "Cor Anglais" Baker of Middle Street

Teltayltit

Anyone identified as a *teltayltit* is certain to be subjected to the disdain and opprobrium of his or her peers. A *teltayltit* is an informer, one who names names, a vile person who sneaks to report to authority figures various acts of mischief perpetrated by his or her schoolfellows. The unwritten code of the Port Isaac County Primary School playground is that tales must never be told on others, irrespective of the personal cost. It is therefore not difficult to appreciate the extent to which *teltayltits* are disliked. The overriding dilemma facing one who has been informed on is that it does him no good at all to go and bash up a *teltayltit*, as that kind of retribution will only result in his being told on again.

"Ah got ayved out uv th' church choir fer theevin a bar uv chocklit frum wan uv th' church windas on Vrahdy aybenin back be arviss festyvill time. Ah took th' chocklit up t' th' peckchurs to share un out with th' buhys, en wan uv they oo dedden git a square mus' uv gone en tol' on me t' th' vicar. Tez sartin nuff oo telled, en tez a reel shaame cuz ah dedden knaw th' bugger wuz a teltayltit."

Temprince

A state of personal grace that, as manifested by a fair number of Port Isaac Bible-thumpers, demonstrates that talking the talk beats walking the walk every time. Most of those who allegedly live in accord with *temprince* tend to follow the Chapel persuasion. The *temprince* stamp requires the shunning of all forms of alcohol-containing beverages other than the contents of a certain resident bottle of strong stuff in the sideboard back at home from which the regular draughts for "medicinal purposes" are poured. A well-known *temprince* motto is **"Our drink be water bright"**—although if an adherent should chance to find himself during opening hours near a pub in which his anonymity will be assured, then *temprince* is likely to be *tempererrily* overcome by *temtaashin*.

"That ol' maid Jinny frum up be th' Post Office come out uv th' baaker's shop en zeed me on me way into th' pub crost th' road. Er be proper chapel Jinny be.

'Ee wun't vind nart no good in there,' er zayed t' me. 'Twood be better fer ee t' folla the way uv Zalvaashin droo a life uv temprince!'

'Mebbe you'm right maid,' ah tol' er, 'but ah kin tell ee wan thing, that th' zeverl pints uv Walter Icks's piss ah be guyne ev in there'll make ee look a lot purtier ef ah meets ee 'gain on the way out!'"

In fond memory of Miss Jinny Hills, a by-word for integrity as Port Isaac's postmistress

Terrubble

Terrubble is a synonym for "very". Hence there is nothing fearful about this word. It must be used with circumspection however, as for example *thank ee terrubble much* could come across to the uninitiated as sounding *terrubble* laboured.

> "*Maake shoo-er ee do put yer ballyclaver en gloves on afore ee gits guyne downtown, tez terrubble cold outzide.*"

Tetty

A tuber which (thank heavens!) crops in the garden in abundance when *teelin* is carried out with the respect that is its due. The *tetty* is the definitive Port Isaac dinner-time food staple. It beats bread hands down for the title of "staff of life". A typical *tetty* just out of the ground is more or less ovoid to spherical in shape—in size it can range from fingernail up to fist dimensions. *Tetties* are cultivated from individual seed tubers laid down at rigidly fixed intervals at the bottom of arrow-straight shallow trenches dug (and subsequently infilled and banked up) in richly *teeled* soil. Considerable after-care is lavished at all stages of the development of the *tetty* crop. Digging up the harvest at the appropriate moment involves a degree of physical labour that may not suit the will of all but the most fervent of gardeners. A reasonably sized *tetty* can make an excellent missile for a boy to throw at both his friends and his enemies. *Tetties* dedicate their excellence to such gems of Port Isaac cuisine as *paasties*, *tetty uddle*, and *tettyenturnup pah*. When boiled, roasted, fried (as chips) or mashed, *tetties* are consumed in their purest state. It is vital that *tetty* skins, which will go on to be eaten by pigs, are finely pared off with a sharp knife. A hole in the heel of a sock exposing an expanse of tidemarked flesh is, thanks to the combined image, known to most Port Isaac boys as a *tetty*.

> "*Up be Sint Androos' Otel on th' Terrice, me mother 'oo do*

work there zayed that fer dinner on a taable with fower people they puts out a baasin' with only dwelve tetties in un t' go round all fower uv em. Dwelve tetties b'tween fower! Ah bleeve thass neer nuff 'bout dree aych! Mah gar, ef ah gits twelve tetties be mezelf on me awn fer dinner ah vinds mezelf lookin' fer moo-er!"

Tez en Tedden

If *tez*, certainty abounds, banishing all elements of doubt as effectively as dull care is prithee begone. Diametrically opposed to this happy state of affairs if *tedden*, another option has to be sought in order to ensure that ultimately *tez* so that *thassuvvun* can truly be declared.

> "Andy, that was a fascinating story, but it surely can't be true?"
>
> "Missis, all ah kin zay ez that ef tedden troo tez valse, though mind ee, ef ah zays tez, then tez, ayben when tedden."

With thanks to Mr Oswald Pryor, cartoonist of Moonta, SA, Australia, and in fond memory of Mr Andy Oaten of Rose Hill

Theevin

An unlawful act in the commission of which certain persons acquire the property of others and assume ownership of the same. They expect to reap the benefits of this *theevin* without feeling a shred of remorse. A rather more acceptable philosophy of *theevin* from the *Likes uv They* in order to hand on the proceeds to the *Likes uv We* vanished with the demise of its legendary perpetrator, Mr Robin Hood. A useful synonym for *theevin* is *whippin*, the root of which is celebrated in the person of Mr Charlie Chester's cat burglar creation, Whippit Kwick, who rose to fame in Charlie's *Stand Easy* wireless programme.

185

"Moses wuz gived den c'mandmints be God. Us ad t' larn em all be 'art in Zundy skool. Th' aytf wan wuz tellin we that us ken't go out theevin. Tez sartin God never comed t' Port Isaac er a wooden uv rote thack on a stone! Ah knaws ol' God wooden in Port mind ee, cuz in th' denf c'mandmint a tol' we not t' covet our nayburrs haass. God kin never uv zeed the zize uv mah nayburrs haass, er a would have thought better uv ut. No bugger could covet thack wan."

They

They are either them or those. *They* are not *we* by any degree of imagination, and you only have to consider the *Likes uv They* as the self-appointed betters of the *Likes uv We* to realise how true this assertion is. The *Likes uv They* are of course invariably more elevated in social standing than the *Likes uv We* can ever aspire to be, but as to the former being superior to the latter there is not a fat rat's chance in Pawlyn's cellars of that happening.

"Lookin' over the cliff wall down be Little 'Ill, ee kin zee all they emmets guyne round en round down on th' baych. Ah dun't jus' knaw what t' think 'bout em, cuz tez the Likes uv They that do bring the kind uv munny down 'ere t' spend that th' Likes uv We ebben got nart uv. Ah s'pose s'long ez the buggers do be spendin' uv ut tez better fit fer ah t' kaype me gob shut."

Thick en Thack

Ideally accompanied with a demonstrative gesture of the hand, (extending the index finger only please), *thick* relates to something or someone that is relatively close to hand and *thack* is invoked to make reference to them when they seem to be a bit further away. As far as *thack* is concerned the distance separating the observer from

186

the subject can in principle stretch all the way out to the horizon. *Thick en thack* can also be used to differentiate between a preference for one thing in comparison to another. The *th* sound in *thick* as well as in *thack* is pronounced in accordance with *th* as in the word "the". *Thicky en thacky* are occasionally brought into conversation as respective substitutes for *thick en thack*. There is no known plural version of either—the task of considering two options simultaneously is about as much as any Port Isaac man can manage.

"'Ere buhy, Ah jus' maade a ayp uv yaiss buns, en they'm still 'ot frum th' uvvin. Ee kin ev thick wan ef ee likes."
"Well reely ah'd zoonner ev thack wan be th' back, what do look as ef a do ev a load moo-er currints in un."

Thot

A broad strut spanning the centre of a punt in a position set marginally below gunwhale level. As well as providing support for the backside of a rower (or rowers) a *thot* incidentally helps maintain overall integrity in the punt's framework.

"Any bugger oo do zay ee shooden rock th' boat ebben never stood on a thot en rocked a punt vitty frum zide t' zide down in th' arbour. Th' vishermen dun't like t' zee ut done, but tez zich a vitty gaame us dun't worry bout they 'cep fer the bugger 'oose punt tez."

Tidy

Since domestic norms in Port Isaac are imbued with a condition owing much to an association with *Lanson Jail,* appreciable neatness and cleanliness tend to be about as easy to find as are proper meat and gravy in the corners of a *boughten* pasty—hence to Port Isaac folk conventionally accepted concepts of keeping the home and hearth tidy are reckoned to be not really worth bothering about.

As a consequence *tidy* has come to mean a reasonable quantity of something or other, and has been just that for a *tidy* number of years.

> "Ah got t' go up t' Endellion s'afnoon. 'Ow long do ee think t'will taake me t' git there ef ah walks on me vit?"
>
> "Well, Endellion do be a tidy way off frum 'ere, but ah do s'pose the time ut taakes ee t' do uv ut kin dee-pend ef ee walks long th' valley paff droo Pennant, er ef you'm guyne up Church 'Ill en then crost th' vields. Then ut do elp t' cut th' ol' time ef ee do maake a tidy paace, en dun't go traipsin' 'long like a foo hours dun't mayne nart to ee."

Timberill

A steeply inclined and oftimes *canvas*-clad stepped route that small boys under parental orders to partake of immediate nocturnal repose ascend both slowly and reluctantly.

> "Now then me ansum, edden ut time ee wuz climbin' up timberill t' git inta blankit alley?
>
> "No tedden! Ah ben't slaypy ait!"
>
> "Jus' do ee git up they bleddy stairs you little bugger you afore I tans yer haass fer ee!"

Titchy

As a characterisation of anything small, the adjective *titchy* is normally applied with a hint of a jibe behind it, in order perhaps to imply that its object could well do with having a little more in the way of stature in order to merit a proper level of respect. A *little tacker* can also be referred to as a *titcher*.

> "Ever'thin 'bout un do be titchy. A do stand only vahve foot nart, en ef a turned zideways in a gaale ee cooden zee un. There edden a zingle gen'riss thought in th' miser'ble ol' 'aid

188

uv a. Titchy en tetchy, thass uv un awright."

In fond memory of a fair few of Port Isaac's coterie of miserable old buggers

To

With no pun intended, this utterly indispensable word has two distinctive meanings in conversation. The more important directs attention to the currently known location of a person, place or thing—providing in effect a declaration on where that person, place or thing is *to*. The second application of *to* relates to something that was formerly open but currently closed—preferably closed as noisily as possible when that something is a door. Slamming a door *to* is the preferred way to ensure closure every time.

> *"When ah come inta th' 'ouse en ayved the back doo-er to, the chaange from buyin' me shoppin' wuz in me ann. Ah put ut down en now ah ken't vind ut nobleddywhere. Tebben bin theeved, zo where th' ell kin ut be to?"*

Traade

All of the material things that you own or have the use of for the commission of your work (with apologies for the inclusion of such a fearsome four-letter word) are your *traade*. When you combine the whole lot under the single title of *traade* you avoid having to make any further effort to list the individual items.

> *"Me brother wuz passin' be Wesslick Brown's 'ouse—the doo-er wuz abroad so a took a gaake in droo un. A zayed that a never zeed s'much deer traade lyin' round anywhere like ut in all a's boo-ern days."*

Traipsin

The well-loved art of ambling or slouching along in a posture

189

indicative of haste not being of the essence, even in the unlikely event that there might have been somewhere important to go to in the first place.

> "Ah do wish ee wood git a bit uv spring in yer vit! You'm traipsin round lookin s'ef ee've los' zeckspince, voun a penny, gone ome, tried to scat the skin off a rice puddin' en cooden do ut."

Traycull

An ultra-thick liquid derivative of sugar, *traycull* flows with all the urgency of a snail climbing up a window pane. *Traycull* is clear, textureless and golden in colour (it says so on the tin) and is expressly intended for consumption by owners of sweet teeth. Also from the legend on the *traycull* tin an ardent reader will observe that out of the strong came forth sweetness. *Traycull* is ideal for—spreading on new bread; mixing in a big whorl in porridge; being licked directly off a serving spoon; infusing a thick layer of breadcrumbs within a pastry base to make a *traycull tart*, and applying with volcanic aplomb to the crown of a steamed sponge pudding. Only the unwise dare to use the so-called *black traycull* as a substitute for proper *traycull*—you may consider yourself duly advised.

> Roobarb tart,
> Maakes ee fart.
> But when th' tart be traycull,
> There do be no aykwull.

Another playground original

Trig

A distinctive item of the fisherman's *traade* assembled from three short pieces of wooden plank sawn to length and nailed together in the form of a right-angled triangle fit to merit the approval of

Pythagoras himself. A *trig* can in principle be of almost any size, although since its manageability is inversely proportional to its dimensions, a typical one tends to come along on a modest scale only. Its wedge-like geometry ensures that a *trig* can be easily shoved or kicked into place under an inherently wobbly object such as a punt or a barrel of herrings lying on its side so as to support and maintain upright stability with the hypotenuse.

> *"You dree buhys 'old thack punt in plaace, en you other pair uv little buggers do ee stand wan on aych zide t'ayve they trigs in under un t'gether so when ee kicks em 'ard t'will maake em both tight."*

Tripplin

As a consequence of stubbing a toe when you are out perambulating, a stumble may occur, causing you to go *tripplin*. It is not unlikely that when you *tripple* you are about to measure your length on the ground.

> *Anna Jones*
> *Broke 'er bones,*
> *Be tripplin over*
> *Cherry stones.*

In fond memory of the fearsome Miss Anna Jones of Trefreock

Turnup

A seasonal root vegetable so popular in Port Isaac kitchens that it is more or less taken for granted. A *turnup* will normally grow to match the size and approximate shape of a human head. It is rounded, solid and compact within a durable purple-streaked skin. When rooted in soil a *turnup* exposes only a portion of its mass to the elements from beneath an umbrella-like burst of protective green leaves. Once a *turnup's* skin has been pared away, the edible flesh beneath will be seen to possess a yellow hue deepened by orange overtones. *Turnup* is often cut up, boiled and mashed in the company of parsnips to accompany the Sunday dinner joint. Finely diced *turnup* is a key ingredient of *tetty en turnup* pie and is also included in *paasties* for those whose taste runs to that sort of thing. A proper *turnup* should not be confused with a *white turnup*, which is much smaller than the former and better eaten raw than cooked.

> "Turn-ups cabb-eedge!
> Turn-ups, cabb-eedge!"

With thanks to Messrs Sam and Will Blake of Trewetha Farm and Mr Bill (Bumps) Masters, their ever-jovial assistant on the vegetable vending round.

Twuz en Twooden

Twuz en twooden are respectively the past tenses of *tez en tedden*. Any Town Platt yarn about what Port Isaac used to be like back in the legendary realm of the "good old days" generally gains so much in its telling and retelling that what is recounted is often too close to call irrespective of whether or not *twuz er twooden* true.

> "Ol' Tom sent we up to a's cellar t' git a ole what a tol' us wuz
> lyin' on wan uv a's shelfs. A wantid we t' bring ut down to un
> zo a could put th' 'ole on the wall t' look droo en zee ef t'wuz
> rainin' outzide er not. S'far ez th' shelf went, us vound the
> bugger, but as fer th' 'ole, twooden there 'tall."

With further thanks to Mr Tom Brown, whose famous cellar shelf also held a tin of black and white striped paint and a left-handed screwdriver.

192

U

Uckin

Uckin is the standard procedure by which foreign matter (chiefly consisting of fluff or dust or grime blended with organic secretions) is evacuated from various of the body's orifices and epidermal creases. The practice of *uckin* calls for assiduous probing of the said declivities with either the fingers or an appropriately pointed object held firmly in the *ucker's* grasp. Based on anticipated yield the best locations for *uckin* are the earholes; the outer nasal cavity; the gaps between one's remaining teeth and any incidental cavities; the navel (or belly button); the anus (or asshole for those who, unlike *Cafflick* priests prefer not to use Latin words); between the toes; and under the fingernails. *Uckers* know that not all of their endeavours are going to meet with success as measured by the quantity of matter they eventually retrieve, yet they are equally aware that any disappointment is sure to be compensated by the immense satisfaction of sooner or later fortuitously *uckin* out something large enough to be examined, sniffed, and tasted.

> *"When we ev's a jynt uv bayfe fer Zundy dinner, faather do spend all uv* Fambly Faavrites *en mos' uv th'* Billy Cotton Band Shaw *tryin' t' uck the stringy bits out frum a's teef with a matchstick."*

193

Uddle

In the unlikely event that any *tetties* succeed in surviving a Port Isaac dinner time to become transformed into left-overs, their destiny will be to contribute to the dinner time of the following day, when in all probability they will be blended into a concoction bearing the evocative name of *uddle*. The recipe for *uddle* is simplicity itself—(a) left-over *tetties* are dissembled into small pieces and placed in a large cast iron frying pan together with a little water and a few shakes of salt and pepper; (b) a large onion is peeled, sliced and added to the contents of the frying pan; (c) a strip or two of fat bacon (if available) is additionally thrown in; (d) the frying pan is placed over heat and the ingredients are stirred around until they combine into a featureless mush; (e) the mush (*uddle*) is portioned out onto individual plates with the help of a wooden spoon; (f) the *uddle* is eaten, sometimes with relish and sometimes with resignation; (g) any residue left on the plate is mopped up with new bread; (h) the plate is licked clean enough to be put away without washing.

> *"Whabbee us evin' fer our dinner?"*
> *"Us be guyne ev tetty uddle."*
> *"Bugger me ef us dedden ev th' zaame thing esterdy!"*
> *"Aiz, en ef ee dun't ayt whass put uv ee 'day ee'll be aytin' tetty uddle morra s'well! Ev ee fergot there do be a war on?"*

With many thanks to Mr Jim (Granfer) Creighton of Canadian Terrace

Ugly

Relates to any aspect of either a person or a thing that a beholder envisages as being (for example) incomplete, nasty, slipshod or unrepresentative of not only quality but also value for money. There really is a *purty* lot of people and *traade* that might well be described as *ugly* in Port Isaac—a sentiment with which no doubt *Mr 'Arry*

Frampton would concur.

> "*Whass ut like th' way er do dress erzelf? Ayben when tez Zundy er comes t' th' bleddy church lookin' like a zack uv shit tied up ugly.*"

Up th' line

A one-way excursion undertaken, following the order of a magistrate or a judge and allegedly at the pleasure of the British Monarch, by someone whose protestations of innocence have gone unheeded. At the eventual destination secure and gratis bed and board for the one-way traveller is provided for a period of time sometimes measured in years and during which all travel options are so restricted that an "Alfie Hinds" method of exit is always worth consideration. To add insult to injury both the identity and misdeeds of far too many of North Cornwall's miscreants who get sent *up th' line* are reported in lip-smacking detail in the pages of the *Gardyin.*

> *Eenie meenie minie mo,*
> *Caitch ol' Charlie be a's toe,*
> *Ef a's bad, a's off be rail*
> *Up th' line t' Bommin jail.*
> *Ef a's good, let un go,*
> *Eenie meenie minie mo.*

Ut

The third person pronoun which, in the company of *a* (or *un*) and *er* (or *she*), helps to make a vital trio of words readily applicable to the specification of any person or any thing of any kind. Someone (of either sex) who merits being classified as a *miser'ble bugger,* may justifiably be referred to as *ut.*

> "*Ef ut do look like shite, ef ut do smell like shite, en ef ut do veel like shite, tez sartin that ef ee taastes ut tez guyne be shite fer shoo-er.*"

195

Uv

The pronunciation of *uv* is equivalent to the "ove" in "love"—this is not inappropriate in fact as in essence *uv* means "pertaining to" or "belonging to", and you can't get on more intimate terms with a subject than that. Alternatives which occasionally supplant *uv*, usually voiced by the type of people who see no harm in toying with perfection, are *ub* and *o'*.

> "*Thass mah buhy en a's skool class peckchur standin' over there be th' back raw, deer uv un. A do be vull uv mischeef, but thass buhys fer ee, edden ut?*"

V

Vearns

Vearns are among the most common plants of the hills and valleys of St Endellion parish. In maturity they have a tall, feathery and ethereal appearance. During the springtime of the year *vearns* rise from what has seemed hitherto to be lifeless ground and rapidly take over the terrain in the manner of an invincible army. Then, when the cold touch of autumn fingers across the shadowy land the *vearns* collapse and expire in a tangle of crackling brown stalks. Referred to as "bracken" in guide books, in late summer prime the cut green fronds of *vearns* form an invaluable medium for lining the sides and base of chip baskets when blackberry picking is in vogue.

> *"Zometimes ah do think that vearns do be no bleddy good t' man ner bayst. Ee ken't ayt em 'cept mebbe a bit when they'm just shootin' up, en ayben then they dun't taaste like nart. En walkin' droo em edden aisy, special when they 'ides th' primrosies—ef ee ben't careful vearns kin give ee a cut wuss'n a raazer when ee do graabold uv em wrong."*

Vedgytibbles

A generic title governing a significant portion of the range of edible produce grown in a garden or an allotment. Since *tetties* and *graynes* are of sufficient importance to considered as a law unto themselves, *vedgytibbles* are conventionally understood to be mainly root-type varieties, among which the following are probably Port Isaac's most popular:

Karrit	Carrot
Turnup	Turnip
Passnup	Parsnip
Baytroot	Beetroot
Raddeesh	Radish
Marra	Marrow
Layke	Leek

It is from *vedgytibbles* like these that dinner time gets blessed with a degree of blandness that is as complete in itself as is the way in which a Port Isaac man knows his place in society.

> "*Th' objicks that Normin 'Ackforth do tell we 'bout en zaycrit on Dwendy Kweschins all be ayther annymull, vedgytibble, min'rul er abstrack. When wan uv em be vedgytibble we never do 'ear naames like karrits er turnups er things like they fer th' objick en ah dun't knaw why. Ef they wuz t'ev a reel vedgytibble objick, th' Likes uv We could guess un vaster'n Jack Train, Nona Winn, Daphne Perdell en Richerd Dimbleberry all put t'gether, cuz we do graw uv 'em in th' gardin and knaws th' naames be art.*"

Vish

A name associated with an ample variety of species of streamlined marine creatures characterised by a slick-scaled skin, a device known as gills that permits breathing under water, and a prominent arrangement of tail, dorsal and ventral fins which work in concert to promote rapid directional and/or evasive movement. Many *vish* like to congregate in vast numbers in what are known as *skools*, although the individuals in this type of *skool* have nothing to worry about as far as being forced to study *subjicks* is concerned. With net, hook and line fishermen endeavour to catch as many *vish* as they can—*vishin* may not be a particularly moral business but it's what those buggers do and it's a living. A few of the common species of *vish* taken by the Port Isaac fishing fleet are:

Mackerl	Mackerel
Errin	Herring
Pelchurds	Pilchards
Gurnet	Gurnard
Doag	Dogfish
Pollick	Pollock
Plaace	Plaice

"*Ee ken't bayte a vresh mackerl buhy, took right frum th' zay en ayved inta th' ol' vryin' pan fer a foo mineets then out on yer plaate with a gurt 'unk uv noo braid on th' zide.*"

"*Dun't ah knaw ut buhy, mackerl do be the bess kind uv vish on th' taable.*"

Vit

Virtually all Port Isaac people are born with a pair of *vit* (the singular of which is *voot*) one of which is located on each of the lower extremities of their legs. It is normal for two such *vit* to be retained by an owner for the duration of his or her natural life. As appendages, *vit* are not always attractive in appearance, which is probably why they tend to get hidden from sight inside boots and shoes. They do however represent a critical element of support for things like (a) standing up; (b) walking and running: (c) shoe and sock manufacturers; and (d) participation in ass-kicking contests. Each *voot* typically comes along fitted with five *toze* which are to the *vit* what *vingers* are to the *anns*, except that *toze* are shorter and less easy to access for counting with than are *vingers*. On the other hand *toze* are indispensable tools for teaching babies about which little piggy either went to market, stayed home, had roast beef, had none or went wee wee wee all the way home. Other features of a *voot* are: a *zole* on the underside; an *eel* at the rear for wearing out socks; and an instep on the top on which a ring-like tidemark of honest dirt laps just in behind the *toze*. A *voot* is also the word for a formal imperial unit measure of length, although as it happens it would take an awful lot of that sort of *vit* strung together one after the other to amount to any significant distance.

> *"Tez time fer ee t' git up en git guyne down skool on th' vit that God gived ee! Ef ee dun't git guyne zoon ah shull zet wan uv me awn vit t' yer haass!"*

In fond memory of Mr Harry Morman, the cobbler of Church Hill

Vitty

When something is deemed *vitty* it is: fit for purpose; acceptable; well done; and able to be judged at least not bad and at best excellent. In short, *vitty* is applicable where superlatives are concerned. In point of fact *vitty* verges some way towards replacing *proper* as the paramount declaration of a feeling of total satisfaction having been achieved. The difference between *vitty* and *proper* is that whereas the latter must always imply the highest standard, the former can often get away with being *neer nuff*.

> *"Now that Advint Zundy ev come en gone us ev 'ad th' fust bunch uv carol zingers long be th' back doo-er s'aybenin. They zinged "We Dree Kings uv 'Olly en Tar" en ah do tell uv ee, ut zoundid vitty. Mind ee, like mother zayed, they wooden zackly en toon wuz em mother? We gived they a dreppny bit after wan uv 'em 'ammered on th' ol' doo-er, but th' way they*

little buggers kicked the gaate to when they coosed off maade
ah think t'wood ev bin better fit we'd uv gived em zeckspince."

Vurriner

Closely connected to **runner-in, vurriner** is a title of categorisation applied to any stranger (especially one with a curious spoken accent) who enters within the figurative gates of St Endellion parish. Irrespective of whether or not the ultimate motive of a **vurriner** is to reside locally or merely make a short visit to observe Port Isaac characters at work and at play, a **vurriner** he is and a **vurriner** he will remain. If he elects to settle in the parish he does so in a fortunate state of blissful ignorance that it will take a minimum wait of half a century for him to live down his **vurriner** stamp in order to reach the point when he and his descendants merge into the *Likes uv We.*

> *"Oo be that over there, Bill?"*
> *"Tez a bleddy vurriner, you!"*
> *"Ayve a daid rat et th' bugger!"*

With thanks to *Punch* (1854)

W

Waishin

There is no doubt that the frequency with which Port Isaac people carry out their personal ablutions via the regular application of soap and water to the skin is, like the report of Mark Twain's death, subject to exaggeration. Cleansing the body is by dint of long-standing tradition performed by the populace with substantially less diligence than Port Isaac housewives accord to the laundering of clothes and bedding. Although the act of *waishin* can be applied either to the person or to these textiles, *waishin, sensu stricto*, best fits an apparel and bedsheets association. *Waishin* in its pure form is a once-a-week activity, and the day in question, Monday, is as sacrosanct as if it was carved as a commandment on a tablet of stone, with no heed paid to weather conditions. The products of *waishin* are hung up in a sodden row on a rope line stretched between two rickety posts out in the back garden. The technique of *waishin* requires rather a lot of boiling water; the input of much scrubbing using a stiff brush and a bar of hard soap; and the ever indispensable addition of some Reckitt's Blue. *Waished* clothes are *rung out* to get rid of as much retained water as possible (*ringin out* sheets is a two-person job) before being pegged on the line, as it wouldn't do for the *waishin* to be too heavy overall for the poor old length of rope to support. Modern aids to *waishin*, such as a copper installed in the *waishouse* with a great mangle at its side, offer the housewife an advantage. Hazards facing *waishin* on the line are rain (naturally), too much wind or too little breeze, falling gullshit (said by some to bring good luck but not when it splatters a newly laundered sheet) and drifting smuts emanating from cottage chimneys.

> "Waishin day do go vitty zince us ev 'ad th' copper put in, en th' bleddy Kwop zold we that noo waishin powder what they calls dee-ter-gint. Now when th' waishin be done, us kin taake th' 'ot water out frum th' copper in buckits so's they oo want's ut kin ev a baath afower th' vire. There edden many taakers fer baathin' on Mundys though buhy!"

Waiter

A *waiter* is the more prized of the two important commercial species of crab* caught by fishermen in the crabpots they **shet** along the coast of Port Isaac Bay. The hard, crisp top of a *waiter's* smooth oval-shaped shell is russet-brown in colour, whereas on the more vulnerable underside the tone is a pale creamy-yellow. The key characteristic of a *waiter* is a great pair of ever-threatening black-tipped claws, which any fisherman, subject to **nickin** them, ignores at his peril.

> "Be rights frum the pots we'm only s'posed t' taake cock waiters er 'en waiters what ebben got no aigs, then ayve any 'ens with aigs back in th' zay. Losin they 'ens dun't put a loaf uv braid on th' taable fer no bugger though. What we does ez t' scraape th' aigs off th' 'ens zo they oo buys 'em frum we edden none the wiser."

*The second type of crab is called the **spider crab** owing to its appearance in which long and spindly legs radiate from a tight, heart-shaped, reddish rough-backed shell.

Walter Icks's Piss

Let us all praise Mr Walter Hicks, the grand master of the St Austell Brewery, whose proprietary range of ales are purveyed across the bars of a plethora of public houses in Cornwall tied to the purveyance of his products. Not least among this pub pantheon stands Port Isaac's Golden Lion, boasting plentiful regulars who, through lack of choice, are utterly devoted to the copious consumption of Mr Hicks's best and worst alike. Mr Hicks's profession may not appeal to the followers of the temperance movement or for that matter to all Chapel die-hards, but the mighty host of imbibers of his ales never fail to do the great man honour, even down to christening his mild and bitter products on draught with the affectionate sobriquet of *Walter Icks's Piss* and by using that very name to request a pint of the same from their genial landlord.

> *"After dree pint uv Walter Icks's piss, ah do be moo-er'n reddy t' git down t' th' pissouse en git rids uv a couple pint uv me awn broo."*

In fond memory of the Golden Lion's landlord Mr Harry Irons

Way

If someone or something is not here then he, she or it must have gone *way* and therefore be somewhere else. In a reference to football pools results that will be instantly appreciated by the public bar clientele of the Golden Lion, *way* is also the opposite of *ome*.

> *"Where've ee bin buhy? Ah ebben zeed ee fer zum time now!"*
>
> *"Aw, ah bin way."*
>
> *"Where to zackly way?"*
>
> *"Twuz up t' Bood where me zister do live. Er wuz wantin' me t' come 'long en live with er, but doin thack wooden do no good fer me 'tall."*

204

*"Mah gar buhy, ah dun't blaame ee! Ah bin wance up t'
Bood en there edden nart there fer th' Likes uv We be there?
Ah knaws yer zister s'well, en ef ee wuz t'ask me, er do be moo-
er mouthy in Bood than er ever wuz in Port!"*

Waybridge

A large market town situated astride the River Camel at the
approximate upstream limit of tidal reach a few miles above the
estuary at Padstow. As if to justify its name, *Waybridge* is entered,
by those who travel in on the bus from Port Isaac, across a narrow
mediaeval road bridge spanning the river. The width of the bridge
favours horses and carts, and does a very good job of hampering
the two-way passage of such motorised traffic as there is today.
The bridge foundations are legendarily reputed to consist of
appropriately impounded sacks of wool, in celebration of which a
public house named The Bridge on Wool can be found (and visited)
in the *Waybridge* town centre. *Waybridge* is nine miles from Port
Isaac by road (and bus) and is also served by the Southern Railway
with connections to termini at both Padstow and, via Port Isaac
Road station, to Waterloo in London. In addition, a branch railway
line runs from *Waybridge* to Bodmin and parts beyond through
linking up with the Great Western Railway at Bodmin Road station.
Waybridge is additionally blessed with a cinema renowned for daily
performances with a change of programme twice per week. All in all,
Waybridge is not a bad place to go to for a look around, to do some
shopping and to have your dinner at Lang's Fish and Chip shop
before—provided you don't miss it—the bus takes you home again.

*"What time do th' bus layve fer Waybridge buhy?'
"A'll be off jus' s'zoon ez a gits ere."
"Aiz but when be that?"
"T'will be when tez! Why do ee want t' go t' 'Bridge anyhow?"*

In fond memory of the Prout Bros omnibus services of Trelawny Garage,
Port Isaac.

205

We

We, the plural of *ah*, means "us". Its great claim to fame is enshrined in the glorious concept of the *Likes uv We*. It should be noted in passing that the Queen, who lives *up th' line* in a palace in London, is prone to refer to herself as *we* rather than *ah* when she deigns to address her subjects. As the Queen is most definitely one of the *Likes uv They*, such regal misuse of *we* is difficult for the *Likes uv We* to properly appreciate, since as a rule her pronouncements tend to be as far removed from our world as they possibly can be short of them falling off the edge.

> *"Vaar frum th' maadin' crowds ignoble strife*
> *Our zober wishes nivver larned t' stray.*
> *All 'long th' cool zeekwester'd vaale uv life,*
> *We kep' th' nyseliss tenner uv our way."*

With thanks to Mr Thomas Gray

Wessly

An evocative proper noun imbued with a resonance that defines not only Chapel people but also the austere places of worship where they put their self-serving piety so effectively on display. *Wessly* is derived directly from the surname of the brothers John and Charles Wesley, each one an eternal founding pillar of the Methodist establishment and an incidental preacher, musician, author and hymn composer extraordinary. *Wessly* or Chapel, this rose by either name carries enough thorns to ensure that those who lay their hands on it will encounter pricks.

> *"Port do ev doo chapels, wan naamed Wessley up in th' valley, en th' t'other called Skarrick cuz a's down crost from Pawlyn's be th' bottom uv Skarrick 'ill. They'm a vitty pair uv congreegaashuns with a gurt distaaste fer aych other, en nivver th' twain shall mayte in zarvice."*

206

Whitewaish

A stark white liquid, thicker in consistency than milk but not nearly as solid as a good spoonful of skimmed-off cream. A coat of *whitewaish* protects the exterior walls of the home cottage from all the ravages of wind and weather. *Whitewaish* is slopped onto these walls with the aid of a broad and relatively soft-bristled brush wielded (as often as not) by someone who was suffering from a deficit of expertise if the secondary splatter over much of the immediate surrounds is anything to go on.

> *Notiss*—*Nex' Toosdy, bein' Ash Wensdy, there be guyne be a opin air maytin in th' vestry. Th' church c'mitty's guyne be pree-zydid over be a gen'lemin/laady zittin' be wan coorner uv th' roun' table, en the c'mitty be guyne try en dee-zide what colour th' church'll be whitewaished.*

With thanks to Miss Betty Creighton of Canadian Terrace

Winda

An orifice intentionally built into a wall, as for example the wall of a cottage. A *winda* is customarily rectangular in shape and usually comes along complete with a more or less adequately fitted wooden framework infilled with pieces of glass known as *payns* which are secured into the frame by a pleasantly smelling pliable substance named *putty*. Front *windas* are intended to facilitate the ability of cottage dwellers to spy on the activities of their neighbours from a place of concealment behind curtains specially hung and draped for that very purpose. The curtains have the additional benefit of restricting any opportunity for the said neighbours on the outside to observe what is happening on the inside. Provided a *winda* has not been rendered permanently shut owing to its wooden components becoming warped or through an over-zealously layered acccumulation of several generations of paint, it plays a further key role in allowing fresh air to enter the home while at the same time permitting domestically generated odours to escape in the opposite direction. Should a *winda* fail to open naturally it doesn't matter anyway since as a rule in Port Isaac one or more of the *payns* is likely to be broken.

> *"When be ee guyne git off yer haass en clayne th' bleddy windas outside?"*
>
> *"Oo do ee think ah be, George Formby?"*

Winnard

Someone who by appearance looks even more glum than is usual in Port Isaac, or who is otherwise unaccountably morose, utterly forlorn, or all of the above at the same time, qualifies to be described as a *winnard*. All things are relative of course—a hang-dog face categorised as *lookin' like a wet week* passes as normal in a majority of the *Likes uv We* and as a consequence picking out the genuine *winnards* among us requires a fair amount of expert judgement.

> *"Arthur en a's missis wuz s'much at aych others drawts when they wuz t'gither that twuz a wonder wan er tother uv em dedden git up en layve ome. Then 'er passed 'way en wuz took up t'Endellion, en ever zince Arthur uv looked t' be a proper bleddy winnard. There dun't be no countin fer taaste do there?"*

Wisht

When, like the lugubrious comedian Reg Dixon on *Worker's Playtime* you are proper poorly, and yet for all that are stoically still on your feet and up and about doing the best you can to raise a laugh, you are said to look *wisht*. Being *wisht* gives you the freedom to release an unbridled fount of self-pity in which you can wallow and luxuriate while setting out in loving medical detail the history of every last ailment incurred by you in at least the last decade. Once you have been *wisht* for long enough to bore most of your listeners rigid, your upgrade to the condition known as *fayled* is sure to follow.

"Ah wuz up t' Endellion dree day back fer Granfer's foonral. Th' wind wuz blawin' terrubble ez us wuz all stood roun' th' graave en th' vicar's surpliss wuz flappin like a bit uv waishin on th' line while th' zleet wuz comin at we like naydles. Ah look'd et they oo wuz there en zeed 'ow wisht zeverl uv em wuz lookin' en ah thought t' mezelf ah thought, t'wun't be long buhys afore zum uv ee'll be up 'ere t' kaype Granfer cump'ny."

In fond memory of Mr Samuel (Uncle Sam) Honey of Tintagel Terrace.

Withies

Lovely long wands of flexible willow, harvested in annual profusion from specially pollarded trees in garden plantations up in the valleys, *withies* are a perennially renewable resource sustained in their culture by the expertise (of which there is no shortage) of Port Isaac fishermen. A *withy* tree thrives in wetness, in which respect it is not unlike those fishermen who pare off the individual *withies* in season and bind them up in great bundles with tarry twine for transport on their guernsey-clad shoulders down to the cellars at the Town Platt. Once there, the *withies* are trimmed of remnant greenery, graded for thickness and length and carefully selected for weaving into crab pots and *mawns* using a technique handed down through generations. In Port Isaac's principal *withy* garden set in the great mill pool of the Port Isaac valley, monumental *withy* tree stumps, each as tall as a fisherman and broader than the compass of a pair of arms, stand mutely shorn after the annual harvest, each topped with what resembles a gnarled and bristling giant fist, ready to start pushing out the next *withy* crop when the season commands.

"Th' very bes' maaker uv withy pots that Port ever zeed wuz ol'

Tom Brown. Twuz like majeek t' waitch un flippin' en bendin'
they withies t' shaape, en t' zee the pots uv un vormin' up like
maasterpayces all uv em, aych wan garinteed t' breng th' crabs
en lopsters in t' ayt th' skivvered gurnet bait."

Wondered

It is an incontrovertible fact that Port Isaac is full of wonders, and
not the least of these is that it's a wonder that anyone should think
that such an assertion holds water. Be that as it may, it is probably
fitting that one who is *s' wondered* is one who is rather surprised. To
be *not s' wondered* implies that one holds a firm belief in something
that others choose to express scepticism about.

> "*Tez lookin' terrubble black out zay. Dun't look vitty,*
> *though zum zay it dun't mayne nart. Do ee think there do be*
> *a starm comin' in?"*
> "*Buhy, ah wooden be 'tall s'wondered ef t'wooden blawing a*
> *gurt gaale up Middle Strayte be tay time."*

Wood overcoat

A custom-made, all-encompassing wooden box with a matching lid
and fixed brass handles, all of which were precisely assembled by
a carpenter to suit its intended resident's occupant's post-mortem
state of repose as measured by an undertaker. Constructed from
specially chosen timber, the style and cut of a *wood overcoat* can be
either ornate or plain. Its cost reflects the type and quality of the
timber used. When the dearly departed has been laid out within
his or her *wood overcoat* and the lid has been tightly screwed down,
its ultimate resting place will be at the base of a pit of appropriately
sized cross-section excavated to a depth of six feet by the vicar's
operative who holds the rank of sexton. And there the *wood overcoat*
will remain. For ever and ever amen.

"When you'm gone, not only do 'em scroo ee down enzide uv
a wood overcoat t' git rid uv ee, they goes on t' bury ee under
zecks vit uv sile en ayves a bleddy gurt stone on th' top uv ut t'
maake shoo-er ee ben't never guyne come up gaane."

With many thanks to Mr Jim (Granfer) Creighton of Canadian Terrace

Wreck

Wreck is anything at all of a non-marine origin that the sea offers
up to coast dwellers, whether it is found floating on the surface
of the sea (flotsam) or cast ashore by the surging tide (jetsam).
Wooden items dominate the nature of *wreck* picked up along the
coast of Port Isaac Bay, with the most common discoveries being
bits of driftwood, pit props, lengths of planking, fragments of ship
superstructure and great timber baulks in various stages of decay,
waterlogging and barnacle infestation. Other forms of *wreck* that
are less frequently encountered are lengths of rope, cordage and
netting, cork and glass floats and occasionally (with a bit of luck)
useful bits of lost ships' cargo. The unwritten law of *wreckin* practice
is that finders are keepers—when *wreck* has been carried up above
the maximum reach of high tide its ownership is deemed to be
sacrosanct. The national "Receiver of Wreck" and his coastguard
minions disagree with this appreciation of what is right, but the
Likes uv We have got the measure of those miserable buggers and
are more than a match for them.

"Wance a big onshore storm be over, en ah tell ee us do ev
more'n nuff uv they where we lives, tez a good time fer guyne
out 'long the cliffs t' look fer wreck. When th' wreck wood we
finds gits dry tez good fer th' vire, though ut do maake th' ol'
flaames go braave en yeller."

211

X

X-muss

An alternative name for the magnificent festival of *Chrissmuss*, although according to what the vicar says, *X-muss* should live forever in infamy. The vicar doesn't care for *Chrissmuss* to be spoken of or written down as *X-muss* at all. In no uncertain terms he told the boys at Sunday school that using an *X* in place of *Chriss* is "an objectionable invocation of the symbol of the cross." There were a few boys who agreed with him, but most of us didn't know what the *bleddy* hell he was talking about. All in all, *Chrissmuss* comes to be anticipated but once a year and enjoyed for the time that is in it whatever anyone chooses to call it. There are not many Port Isaac boys who want to see too much religion being brought into *Chrissmuss* though. We get more than enough religion shoved down our throats in church and chapel every Sunday to want to spoil a celebration like *Chrissmuss* or *X-muss* with any more of that sort of carry on. In deference to the vicar however, let us consign *X-muss* to the outer darkness where the bugger thinks it rightly belongs and focus our minds on *Chrismuss*. How better to do just that than to sing some carols!

Us Dree Kings

Us dree kings uv 'olly en tar,
Wan in a taxi, wan in a car.
Wan on a scooter, blowin' a's 'ooter,
Follerin' yonder star.

With many thanks to the Rev J. H. Hopkins

Good King Wencissliss

Good King Wencissliss look'd out
On th' fayst uv Stephen.
Turned a's twowsis inside out
T' kaype a's haass frum frayzin.

Zur, a lives a good layg 'ence
Undernayth th' mountin.
Standin' be th' forest fence
Pissin' like a fountin.

With many thanks to Mr John M Neale

Ark! Th' Erald Aangels

Ark! Th' 'erald aangels zing,
Beecham's Pills be jus' th' thing!
Ef ee wants t' go t' eb'n,
Ee ev t' taake zecks er zeb'm.
Ef ee wants t' go t' 'ell,
Ee got t' taake th' box s'well.
Ark! Th' 'erald aangels zing,
Beecham's Pills be jus' th' thing!
Ark! Th' 'erald aangels zing,
Beecham's Pills be jus' th' thing!

With many thanks to Mr Charles Wesley

Y

Yayss

A wondrous compound with a damp, crumbly texture that is pleasantly cloying to the touch. In its raw *boughten* state the smell of *yayss* is most agreeable—a small quantity placed in the mouth provides a taste that is more than tolerable. As an essential ingredient in the preparation of bread and saffron cake, *yayss* incorporates the magic to make the dough rise, thereby being instrumental in ensuring that the final product out of the baking oven ought to have a bare minimum of jawbreaking characteristics.

> *"Th' vicar down be Zundy skool tol' we that in th' Bahbull yayss be knawn ez leb'm. Ah thought leb'm wuz a number, wan moo-er'n den, but ah s'pose th' bleddy vicar d'knaw bess."*

Yer

In the context of time and location, otherwise known as the here and now, it is permissible to use *yer* as an alternative for *ere* (although the latter is to be preferred). *Yer* finds its forte as a buttonholing device, a word cast as a hook to catch someone's attention. *Yer* as heard in Port Isaac can be taken to offer a succinct summing up of the intent that Mr William Shakespeare probably had in mind when in *Julius Caesar* he made Mark Anthony proclaim "Friends, Romans, countrymen, lend me your ears!" The verbal approach of Port Isaac people, for all that it is circuitous, still tends to be a little more direct than that relating to the Bard of Avon, so that **yer buhy** as an attention grabber serves the purposes of the *Likes uv We* very well. Of course since a majority of the *Likes uv We* count themselves fortunate if they get passed the time of day when they meet someone, being lent a pair of ears would never appear in the cards of any hand they would expect to be dealt.

> *"Yer, ah s'pose a wooden all that baad a man reely."*
>
> *"Reely? Yer buhy, ah dedden come up t' Endellion t' praise that miserble ol' bugger—ah be 'ere t' zee un buried good en daype! There edden no goodniss guyne down with un in a's bleddy wooden overcoat!"*

With many thanks to Mr William Shakespeare

You

An appendage to spoken comments and observations that gets used with great, some would say over-repetitive, frequency. Foreigners, who are never quite in the picture, tend to view the terminal **you** as redundant inasmuch as it doesn't appear to alter the substance of its precedents by as much as a **skerrick**. All proper Port Isaac men know, however, that the great value of an appended **you** is vested in the weight it adds to what was said, since by implication it draws in the person of the listener. **You** can be satisfactorily substituted for **buhy** or **maid** at the end of a sentence at any time.

> *"Ah 'eard that ee bin workin' down be th' clayworks buhy."*
>
> *"Aiz, ah startid 'bout a wayke back you. Me job be t' shovel way th' ol' clayey shite! We'm up t' th' naze en th' bleddy stuff down there! Ah dun't think ah be guyne kaype ut up fer much longer."*
>
> *"You'm right. Life be too shart fer that you!"*

215

Z

Zaame

Things that look alike, or appear to be equivalent to one another or which have an overwhelming number of individual similarities in a broad brush comparative sense—much as one piece of rounded shingle down on the Port Isaac harbour foreshore resembles another piece—are said to look the *zaame*.

> *"They local praychurs, they all tells we the zaame ol'thing ever' time. Any pair uv they buggers be like doo chaykes uv th' zaame haass"*

Zackly

Precisely. *Zackly* is so much a fellow-traveller of precision that as a matter of principle its use suggests that no margin of comparative difference exists, because if it did exist it wouldn't be tolerated. That at least is the general idea, more or less, give or take a bit here and there when push comes to shove and so on and so forth.

> *"Now then, 'ere be th' cleckshin baigs frum s'aybenins zarvice! Ah wants ee t' count ut all up and tell th' mount clecktid zackly in pouns, shellins en coppers, though ah dun't specks us be*

guyne git much in th' way uv pouns! Better t' count un up dree
times t' maake shoo-er ee gits un zackly right."

"Well 'ere tez then. Ah dun un dree times like ee zayed en
got un zackly deffernt aych time fer ee."

In fond memory of Mr John Neal, St Peter's church warden

Zaffern

A glorious spice with a unique fragrance without which a *zaffern*
caake would be no better than an ordinary *yayss caake*—not that
any Port Isaac boy worth his salt would refuse the offer of a slice
of either. The dusky red, finely ethereal and wispy filaments that
constitute *zaffern* are stamens taken from a species of crocus and
commercially dried. It requires only a tiny pinch of *zaffern* steeped in
water to liberate the distinctively yellow colouration and brilliantly
subtle flavour that places a *zaffern caake* at the very pinnacle of the
cake league table.

> *"Ee dun't git moo-er'n neerly nart fer yer coppers when ee do*
> *buy a paaper uv zaffern, but tedden all that ut do zeem t' be,*
> *cuz where zaffern be consarned jus' 'bout bugger all uv ut do*
> *go a long way."*

Zalm

The Bible contains a goodly collection of exactly one hundred
and fifty *zalms* set out in order in an Old Testament Book not
inappropriately entitled *Th' book uv Zalms*. This very well rounded
number of *zalms* is entirely consistent with the demonstrated
penchant for orderly numbers of he who carved no more and no less
than Ten Commandments on tablets of stone. Many of the *zalms*
on offer are attributed to the authorship of David—his slaying of
Goliath must have been somewhat motivational. David had the
grace to keep most of his *zalms* mercifully short, in marked contrast

217

to the *zalm* writer who reached rock bottom when he penned the seemingly endless *zalm* number 119. It is no secret that the *zalms* favoured by the St Peter's church congregation in Port Isaac are among the shortest of the century and a half. Although only one of the *zalms* is selected by the vicar to be sung during Matins and Evensong services in the church, the majority of the congregation would much sooner sing a hymn.

Zalm Dwendy-Dree

Th' Lard do be me shep'erd, ah ben't guyne want fer nart.

A do maake me t'lay down in grayne paaschers, a do layd me beezide still waaters.

A do ree-stoo-er me zawl.

A laydith me in the paaths uv rychissniss fer a's naame's zaake.

Aiz buhy, though ah walks droo th' valley uv th' shadda uv Endellion, ah ben't guyne veer no ayvull.

Fer ee do be 'long uv me, yer rod en yer staaf do comfert me.

Ee do maake a taable afore me in th' presince uv a ol' ayp uv miserble buggers what dun't like me.

Ee ev annyntid me aid with ile.

Me cup be runnin' over you.

Shoo-erly goodniss en marcy be guyne t' foller me all th' days uv me life,

En ah be guyne dwell in th' 'ouse uv the Lard forever buhy.

With many thanks to David

Zanzow

The name given to a common (and garden) insect that is more formally known as a woodlouse. Humble in its habits, this insect is a celebrated survivor, thriving in dark, damp and dirt-ridden corners.

It clearly has something in common with many residents of Port Isaac. *Zanzows* like to assemble in large numbers beneath loose pieces of slate, dead vegetation and rogue bits of rotting wood. Their enduring presence around a cottage suggests that the cottage owner is not cleaning the place up as well as he ought to be.

> *"A zanzow do be a emmet 'oo do be'aave like a ayge'og. Ef ee should tap uv 'un with yer vinger, th' fust thing a's guyne do be t' roll up in a titchy ball."*

Zay

Zay is what life in Port Isaac revolves around. Without the mighty expanse of Atlantic *zay* water (and not a drop to drink) to confront, the cliffs of Port Isaac Bay either would not exist or would need to be called something else. The *zay* as a creature is often less than kind. It spreads far and wide out beyond the Bay in its many moods, uniting with the sky at the horizon to mark a virtual rim to the world where, according to some fishermen down on the Town Platt, a ship in the hands of an unwary skipper can easily topple to its doom over the edge. The fishermen go down to the *zay* in boats and occupy their business on its great waters, endeavouring to maximise the catch of whatsoever passeth through the *zay's* paths. In Port Isaac an ocean wave is also referred to as a *zay*, although since one wave never appears without the company of others, it is more common to speak of *zays* in respect of them. Along the fringe of the Bay, where a steady sequence of such *zays* batters to ultimate effect, the greatest respect is accorded to what is known as a *grounzay*, the deep-seated currents of which churn up a welter of bottom sand and seaweed and sweep up the beach in seething *runs* at express train speed. An item of the gear which (among others) characterises a fisherman is a pair of rubber boots made in a choice of knee length or thigh length—these are popularly called *zayboots*.

"Aw, a life on th' oshin waave,
Be better'n guyne t' zay!
Us gits very little fer dinner,
En a bleddy zight less fer tay!"

With many thanks to Messrs Epes Sargent and Henry Russell

Zee

This is what a properly functioning pair of eyes enables you to do in order to realise visions both pleasant and unpleasant. The past tense of *zee* is *zeed*. On taking leave of others it is appropriate to bid them a hearty *"Zee-ee"* if there is a good reason to believe (whether you like it or not) that they will be met up with again before too long.

Us jyned th' naavy
T' zee th' world.
En what did us zee?
Us zeed th' zay!

With many thanks to the incomparable Messrs Irving Berlin and Fred Astaire

Zeverl

Zeverl signifies a number that is greater than a *foo*, rather more than *zome* and quite a lot less than a *ole ayp*. Time spent in pondering on *zackly* how many *zeverl* actually is will be time wasted. Fear not however, at the very mention of *zeverl*, the minds of the native born of Port Isaac will register the precise number at once.

"*Th' ol' zay do be braave en ruff 'day, dun't s'pose there be guyne be much vishin done.*"
"*Well buhy, ah bin jus' now down be th' 'arbour, en ah zeed zeverl boats guyne out zay.*"
"*Mah gar, s'many ez that!*"

220

Zide

When a Port Isaac boy or girl chooses to ignore the reality of his or her origins (be they ever so humble there is no place like them) through adopting airs and graces borrowed from the *Likes uv They* (this kind of thing happens much more often than is popularly imagined), he or she is said to show *zide*. The good people of Port Isaac are ever-ready to forgive the many run-of-mill shortcomings they observe as existing within their own ranks, but the forgiveness of *zide* finds no support or approval at all.

> *"Ah knawed un whan a's haass wuz 'anging out uv a's trowsis, en a's fambly dedden ev a jerry under th' ol' bayd t' piss in. But will ee look at un now? Big job up th' line, big car en big idees. The bugger do be vull uv zide en a dun't want to knaw th' Likes uv We no moo-er."*

Zome

A word that has at least three meanings. As to which of these is which, well as always context is the key:

(1) *Zome*—a cult of old wives whose individual identities are shrouded in anonymity and who allegedly rejoice in holding shared opinions on a range of topics of consummate triviality.

(2) *Zome*—based on first-hand observation, a "how many" estimate invaluable to anyone not well versed in counting.

(3) *Zome*—a prefix used to add emphasis to an adjective when the adjective by itself is felt to not quite measure up to the needs of the moment.

> *"Zome do zay that th' church do belong to be vull fer Ayster mattins. Ah wuz there be th' zarvis, but there wooden many in buhy, no moo-er'n zome along uv me in th' congreegaashun. All th' zaame, the zingin'wuz zome strong, en ut did zound proper. The vicar gits the cleckshin fer a'zelf be the Ayster*

221

sarvissis, zo I specks zeverl stayed 'ome zo ez t' give th' bugger nart."

Zope

A *boughten* substance that commonly takes the form of a small moulded block of a size well able to be contained in the hand, zope is a personal cleansing agent. Certain proprietary brands of *zope* are wrapped in coloured paper. *Zope* is invariably used in association with water (preferably warm water, but you may not always be that lucky) to remove grime from both the person and the clothes that are worn. The Port Isaac standard rules for washing with *zope* and water are (a) it should be done as infrequently as can be got away with; (b) during the week washing should be applied only to those parts (namely the face and hands) that are regularly exposed to the external elements; (c) any commitment to (b) should be undertaken only when the pressure from elders and betters to comply becomes irresistible; (d) a bath in which the body is nominally washed all over should be taken no more than once a week. If all else fails and taking a bath cannot be avoided, *lettinoff* in water can add an element of enjoyment to the otherwise undesirable experience.

> *Wild Shepherds waished their zocks be night,*
> *All zayted roun' th' tub.*
> *A bar uv Zunlight zope come down*
> *En they began t' scrub.*

With many thanks to Mr N. Tate

Here in the late October light
See Cornwall, a pathetic sight,
Raddled and put-upon and tired
And looking somewhat over-hired,
Remembering in the autumn air
The years when she was young and fair –
Those golden and unpeopled bays,
The shadowy cliffs and sheep-worn ways,
The white unpopulated surf,
The thyme and mushroom scented turf,
The slate-hung farms, the oil-lit chapels,
Thin elms and lemon-coloured apples –
Going and gone beyond recall
Now she is free for "One and All."

John Betjeman (1906–1984), "Delectable Duchy"

Lightning Source UK Ltd.
Milton Keynes UK
UKOW051622130812

197481UK00001B/435/P

9 789080 780859